The Kunming Project   昆明合作项目

The Kunming Project: Urban Development in China—a Dialogue

昆明合作项目:
关于中国城市发展的
国际对话

Carl Fingerhuth, Ernst Joos
Editors on behalf of the cities of
Kunming and Zurich

卡尔·芬格胡特、恩斯特·约斯
代表昆明市和苏黎世市主编

Birkhäuser – Publishers for Architecture
Basel · Boston · Berlin

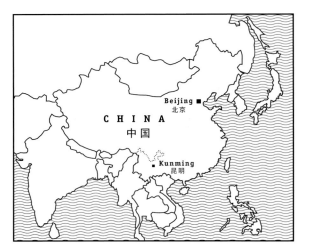

China showing the city of Kunming in the
province of Yunnan.　中国、云南省及昆明市。

LIU XUE AND ZHOU JIE   刘学 周杰

How Kunming Became a Pilot Project 昆明试点项目的回顾

Friendship and Co-operation

When Swiss officials from Zurich visited Kunming in the eighties, they learned of the deteriorating environmental situation of Lake Dianchi and the problems in urban transportation developing in Kunming. Therefore, under the leadership of the Kunming Municipal Government, with the help of the relevant units, different co-operation projects were undertaken, mainly by the Urban Planning and Design Institute. On the Zurich side, under the leadership of Dr. Thomas Wagner, First Deputy Mayor, and through the unified organization and co-ordination of Ernst Joos, general director of projects and deputy director of the Transport Authority, relevant units and professional planners and architects, including Prof. Willy A. Schmid from the Swiss Federal Institute of Technology in Switzerland, visited Kunming several times a year to work on co-operative projects with the relevant departments in Kunming.

Promoting City Planning Theory and Practice in Kunming

The long-term co-operation, exchanges of visits, and discussions between the leaders and people from different strata of Zurich and Kunming created mutual confidence. The Chinese experts learned advanced theory and

友谊与合作

上个世纪八十年代，到昆明访问的苏黎世官员注意到，滇池环境日渐恶化，昆明城市交通环境开始紧张。因此，双方展开了一系列合作项目。在昆明市市政府的领导下，通过有关单位的大力支持，主要由市规划院具体承担了双方合作项目的工作。苏黎世市在市政府第一副市长托马斯·瓦格纳博士的领导下，通过项目总负责人、交通局副局长恩斯特·约斯的统一组织和协调，瑞士及苏黎世有关单位和职业规划师、建筑师，包括瑞士联邦工业大学的威利·施密特教授，每年派出数批技术代表团访昆，与昆明方面对口部门进行合作工作。

对昆明城市规划理论与实践的推动和促进

昆明和苏黎世通过长期合作，以及双方领导和社会各界的互访和交流，建立了相互信赖的关系。中方专家学习了欧洲在城市规划和交通规划方面的先进理论及实践，瑞方专家也逐渐了解了中国国情，双方共同提出的方案具有越来越强的可操作性。现在，昆明市已开通第二条公交专用道，并大力加强二级城市如安宁市的发展，以缓解主城区和滇池地区的环境压力。昆明铁路局也已向铁道部提出申请，

希望改造现有的一段铁路线，以开行
快速市郊列车。

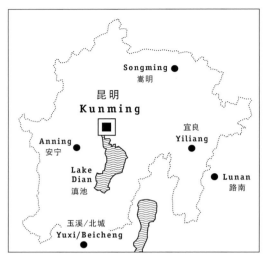

The Greater Kunming Area.　大昆明区。

practice in European urban and transportation planning, while the Swiss experts began to understand China's specific situation, and the schemes proposed together became more and
more feasible. At present, the City
of Kunming built the second line
of bus lanes, is preparing to concentrate its energies on the development of secondary cities like
Anning, with the aim of reducing
the environmental pressure on the
city proper and the area of Lake
Dianchi, and the Kunming Railway
Bureau has finished a proposal for
the Railway Ministry to improve
the first stretch of an existing
line to implement the Rapid Suburban Railway.

合作已取得的主要成果

昆明老城保护项目

由于瑞士专家不断呼吁保护历史文化
名城昆明市的珍贵古建筑，昆明规划
部门最终完成了一批历史街区的保护
规划，并通过了市政府的法律批准程
序。在制订完保护规划的基础上，昆
明市成立了"昆明历史街区与建筑保
护办公室"，专门组织维修昆明市公
房中的历史建筑，并在私房房主维修
其历史建筑时给予指导和支持。目前
这项工作已全面启动，并已取得初步
成果。

Major Results Achieved through Co-operation

The Kunming old town protection project

As a result of continued urging by Swiss experts to preserve the priceless built heritage
of the historically and culturally famous city
of Kunming, the planning departments of
Kunming at last finished protective plans for
several groups of historical street blocks in
old Kunming, which have been approved by
legal procedures by the City Government. On
the basis of the protection plans, the Kunming Historical Street Block and Building
Protection Office was established. This office organises the renovation of city-owned
historical buildings, and advises and sup-
ports private owners willing to renovate historical buildings. At present, this work has
been fully initiated and some initial achievements have been made.

Kunming metropolitan area planning and the use of the Geographic Information System (GIS) in planning

Based on the *Kunming City Comprehensive Plan (1996–2010)*, this project systematically studied the development conditions of Kunming in an international, national and local context. The optimum model for the Greater Kunming Metropolitan Area was brought forth, with the suggestion for a 'network city for the Kunming metropolitan area' with the city proper as the core and a chain of satellite towns built along the existing railway lines. The city proper is to develop moderately, while the development of the satellite towns will speed up. Transportation is based primarily on an intercity suburban railway system to be developed from the current railway. The project includes the implementation of laws and policies. The planning of the Greater Kunming Metropolitan Area was carried out on a scientific and highly efficient basis by plotting the Geographic Information System (GIS) for the whole area and by using satellite photos at 5m resolution.

The project of planning urban public transportation for Kunming

Based on a travel survey and a detailed forecast processed by an international-level advanced computer model, the *Kunming Urban Public Transportation Master Plan* defined the urban traffic policy and the public transportation network for the city proper with a '#'-shaped modern tram line as the backbone, supported by several modern bus lines, all of them to run on a reserved right-of-way on city streets, supported by an advanced traffic management system. Chinese and Swiss experts together finished the *Feasibility Study*

昆明都市地区规划框架及其
GIS规划系统

项目在《昆明城市总体规划（1996－2010）》的基础上，系统地研究了昆明城市发展的国内外及本地区发展条件，提出了最佳模式"昆明都市地区网络城市"。即构成以主城为核心，以沿铁路的一系列卫星城为辅的网络城市体系。其中主城的发展为适度发展，其它卫星城的发展是加快发展。在交通方面，主要依托现已有铁路建立城市间快速市郊列车系统。项目还包括实施有关法律和政策。通过利用5米精度的卫星照片，以及通过建立大昆明地区地理信息系统GIS，大昆明都市地区的规划是建立在科学而高效的基础上完成的。

昆明城市公共交通规划项目

根据居民出行调查和利用具有世界先进水平的电脑模型作出的详细预测，完成了《昆明城市公共交通总体划》。它确定了在昆明主城区以"井"字形城市现代有轨电车为主、以现代公共汽车为辅的公交网络和城市交通政策。所有公交车辆都将行驶在城市道路上的公交专用道上，并将实施先进的交通管理手段支持公共交通。中瑞专家共同完成了"现代有轨电车一号线可行性研究"和"第一条现代公共汽车专用道可行性研究"。昆明市在99昆明世博会前建成了第一条现代公共汽车专用道，承担了世博会大部分游客的交通运输任务。它从通车之日起就获得了巨大成功。

根据欧洲的成功经验，瑞士专家与昆明规划部门和铁路部门的专家经过共同研究，完成了昆明都市地区的"利用现有铁路系统开行快速市郊列车的可行性研究"，进一步提出了对现有

Kunming city proper. 昆明市主城区。

Report on the No.1 Modern Tram, and the *Feasibility Study Report on the First Modern Bus Lane*. The latter was constructed in time to transport the majority of the visitors to the '99 Kunming Gardening Exposition, and was a big success from the beginning.

For the Greater Kunming Metropolitan Area, based on European experiences and the joint research by Swiss and Chinese experts with the Kunming city planning departments and railway departments, a 'Rapid Suburban Railway' feasibility study suggested the use of an improved version of the existing railway system. The study brought forward ideas for the alteration of the existing railway system, and for strategies of suburban train investment and operation. The suggestion was adopted by provincial and municipal leaders and has strengthened the *Network City Plan for Kunming Metropolitan Area*.

The achievements made through co-operation have had an effect not only in Kunming but in other cities in China as well. Three international urban public transportation planning symposia were held in Kunming, and experts from both countries have continuously reported the planning experiences of Kunming in international publications, thus making Kunming more well-known in the world. In 2000, Kunming was listed as one of four Chinese national pilot cities in transportation and environmental treatment. Although the work in Kunming has been recognised domestically by people in the same professions, this is just the beginning. The technical co-operation between Kunming and Zurich will continue to make up-to-date contributions to sustainable city development and transportation policy.

铁路系统的改造工作、市郊列车的投资策略及运营策略等。这项建议深化了《昆明都市地区网络城市规划》中的有关内容，并得到了省政府和市政府领导的认可。

合作的成果不仅在昆明，而且在中国的其它城市也都产生了广泛的影响。在昆明召开了三届"城市可持续发展及公共交通规划国际研讨会"，双方专家也都不断在国际刊物上介绍昆明规划工作的经验，在世界上提高了昆明的知名度。2000年，昆明成为中国四座改善交通与环保综合试点城市之一。虽然工作成果受到了国内专业界的认可，它还只是万里长征第一步。昆明市和苏黎世市的技术合作将继续进行下去，为实现可持续的城市发展和交通政策而作出更大的贡献。

'Spring City', "春城",

rich in tradition, 有着悠久历史,

is in a phase o

apid growth 它如今正经历着飞速发展

and dramatic change. 和深刻变革。

rban development　城市发展建设活动

spills over the historic tow

oundary. 超出了历史上的市区边界。

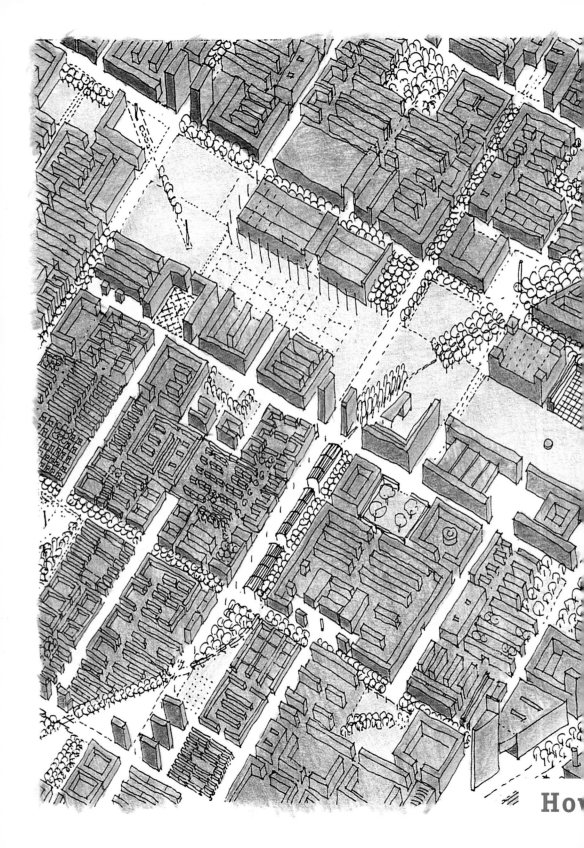

How

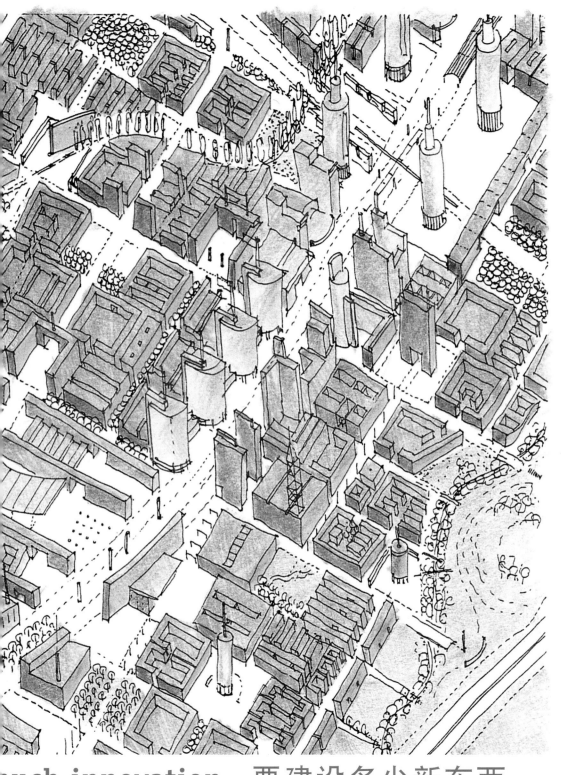

much innovation 要建设多少新东西，

must be made possible 才能满足

EXPO '99
中国昆明

人与自然

云南电力集团有限公司赠

to accommodate new need

...nd values?　人们的新需求和新价值观？

How muc

f the existing 要保留多少现存的东西，

must be preserved　才能使城市

for th

ty to keep its identity 保持它的特色,

and keep its inhabitants 使居民

fro

ecoming homeless?　仍有一种归属感？

清末昆明街道图

Kunming town plan from 1909. The newly built railway station with its still existing narrow-gauge track connection to Hanoi is on the lower right-hand side.   1909年昆明市地图。图上右下方为当时新建的火车站和目前仍保留着的、通往河内的窄轨铁路。

CARL FINGERHUTH   卡尔·芬格胡特

Urban Design for Kunming
昆明的城市设计

Historical Development

In 765 A.D. a small town was founded on the present site [of Kunming] as a fortress against the armies of the Tang dynasty. Its walls were erected directly on the shores of the lake, which today are about 5 km away from this old fortress town. In the 10th century during the kingdom of Dali the town was extended on its west side together with the construction of flood protection and water control works.

When in 1254 A.D. Kubilai, the Mongolian crown prince, conquered the kingdom of Dali a completely new town was built on the ruins of the old town. When the first emperor of the Ming dynasty reorganized the imperial administration the town was rebuilt again with a walled area of about 3 sq. km. The city survived almost unchanged the take-over of the empire of the Manchus in 1682.

Foreign influences arrived in Kunming at the last decade of the 19th century from the south; they were strengthened by the railway line, which connected the city with Vietnam, at that time (1910) the French colony of Indo-China.

(Schinz, Alfred; *Cities in China*, Bornträger, Berlin-Stuttgart, 1989, pp. 291ff.)

In the evening of the fifth day one reaches the splendid imperial capital Jaci [Kunming] where many merchants and craftsmen live. The population is put together of various

历史沿革

公元765年，地方政权南诏国在今天的昆明城区修建了一座小小的拓东城（后改称鄯阐城），抵抗唐朝军队的进攻。当时，拓东城的城墙高高矗立在滇池岸边，现在，滇池距拓东城原址已后退了五公里左右。公元十世纪时，大理国对鄯阐城加以扩建，城区向西扩展，并建设了防洪和水利设施。

公元1254年，成吉斯汗的孙子忽必烈率军平大理国后，在鄯阐城废墟上重建新城。明太祖建立明王朝后，对它再次重建，城墙内的城区规模约为三平方公里。1682年满军攻克昆明时，它几乎没有遭到任何破坏。

十九世纪九十年代，国外的影响从南边逐渐渗入昆明。1910年修筑了昆明至越南（当时为法国殖民地）的铁路后，来自国外的影响进一步扩大。

马可·波罗在他的游记中这样描述昆明：

经过五天的旅行，晚上就到了壮丽的大城押赤（今昆明）。无数的商人和手工业者居住在这里。城里的居民形形色色，有伊斯兰教徒，偶像教徒，还有若干聂斯脱里派之基督教徒。这里有一座方圆一百英里的大湖。湖中鱼儿数量之多，味道之鲜美，都堪称举世无双。人们生吃新鲜的鸡肉、羊肉、牛肉和水牛肉。穷人则到屠宰作坊去，把刚宰杀的动物的肝脏拿回家，趁着新鲜切成薄片蘸蒜汁生吃。

对旧城的处理

古老的昆明

正如生活中的任何现象一样，我们对城市也可作出不同的诠释。我们可以把城市理解为人类社会的大机器：城市为人们提供遮风避雨的场所、把自来水输送到住房里、把污水排走，人员和物资也在城市里流动。

我们也可以把城市看作人们进行社会经济、政治或伦理道德活动所必需的场地。有了城市，才可能进行商业和生产活动、建立国家、贯彻法律。

Workshop held in the Kunming Urban Planning and Design Institute. 在昆明市规划院举办的工作讨论会。

一座城市的外表，还表达了市民们如何理解他们个人及群体的存在方式，以及他们希望向外界展示什么样的自身形象。因此，人们建设气势宏伟的道路和广场，或者遵循风水原理进行建设；也正因如此，人们才决定拆毁或者保护老城。

在我看来，城市的这种复杂性在我们与昆明朋友们的合作中起着决定性的影响。自来水中如果含有过多的大肠杆菌，无论在世界上的哪一处地方，都会威胁人们的生命；在全世界范围内，也都可以用同样的工具测量它的

kinds: there are Mohammedans and heathens and also some Nestorian Chinese. There is a lake of a circumference of a hundred miles. Nowhere on earth would one find more and finer fish. The people eat the raw flesh of chickens, sheep, beef and buffaloes. The poor go to the slaughtering place to collect the liver of freshly slaughtered animals, cut it thinly, dip it into garlic sauce and eat it right away.

(Marco Polo; *Die Wunder der Welt, Bericht von seiner Reise nach China*, written 1298/99, Manesse Verlag, Zurich, 1983, pp. 190ff.)

Dealing with the existing city

The old Kunming

Like all of life's phenomena, cities can be interpreted in many ways. We can explain them as the great machines of human society. Cities serve as protection from rain and cold, bring water to individual flats and take it away again, and facilitate the movement of people and goods.

But we may also understand cities as essential spaces for socio-economic, political or ethical processes. The city enables trade and commerce, the forming of states and the administration of justice.

The city in its physical form is always an expression of the way its population, in their individual and collective humanness, see themselves and want to be seen. This is why they build monumental streets and squares, and have regard for *feng-shui* axes. This is why they destroy old parts of the city or place them under protection.

48

For me, this complexity of the city was the determining factor in our work with our friends in Kunming. Drinking water containing too many Coliform bacteria is a danger to humans all over the world, and can be measured with the same instruments globally. However, dealing with historic buildings or when building a new neighbourhood, global trends and technical experience are superimposed on local cultural and political awareness.

With this in mind we suggested organising our joint work as workshops. I formed a team with experienced urban planners and we met in Kunming twice yearly, each time for two weeks. Chen Xinghua, who was then leader of the urban planning department, chose the topics for the workshops. The urban design tasks themselves were only worked on in Kunming. At the end of each workshop, the authorities in Kunming were presented the results of the joint work in the form of plans and texts, in Chinese and English. These were technically improved in Zurich and assembled into brochures which were then made available to the authorities in Kunming. All illustrations in this article are taken from those brochures.

The urban planning of the Modern Movement was guided by a fascination with a new, supposedly better, city. The old patterns seemed to have become redundant. Order, linearity, transparency, and uniformity were the key-

An historic market street in the old town. 旧城内一条传统的市场道路。

含量。而在处理旧城建筑或者建设新市区的时候，世界上具有普遍意义的发展趋势和技术经验，却都与当地的文化和政治意识交织在一起。

出于这种思想，我们建议用工作讨论会的方式开展双方的合作。我与经验丰富的城市规划师们组成专家小组，每年去昆明访问两次，与昆明的专家们展开合作，每次为期十四天。昆明市规划院当时的院长是陈兴华先生，由他选定我们的研究课题。我们只在访问昆明期间展开昆明城市设计方面的研究。每次工作讨论会结束以后，我们都以文字（中英文对照）和图纸的形式，把双方合作的成果展示给昆明的有关部门。回到苏黎世后，我们再把研究成果进行技术加工，制作成研究报告，并送交给昆明有关部门。本文中的所有插图都来自这些研究报告。

在现代化的城市规划理论和实践中，曾一度推崇建设崭新的城市，人们认为新城优于旧城。旧城的建筑和布局似乎一无用处。严整的秩序、直线性、透明性和整齐划一的风格曾是设计现代化城市的方针。

关于如何处理昆明旧城的首轮研究，起因就是当时要建设从旧城地带横穿而过的人民路，而那时的旧城保存得相当完好。

Fall 1996 年秋

Spring 1997 年春

Fall 1997 年秋

Spring 1998 年春

The construction of Renmin Road from 1996 to 1998, cutting through the old town.
1996年至1998年的人民路建设工程把旧城一分为二。

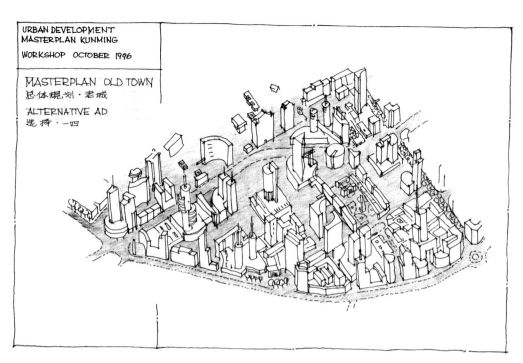

URBAN DEVELOPMENT
MASTERPLAN KUNMING
WORKSHOP OCTOBER 1996

MASTERPLAN OLD TOWN
总体规划·老城
ALTERNATIVE AD
选择·一四

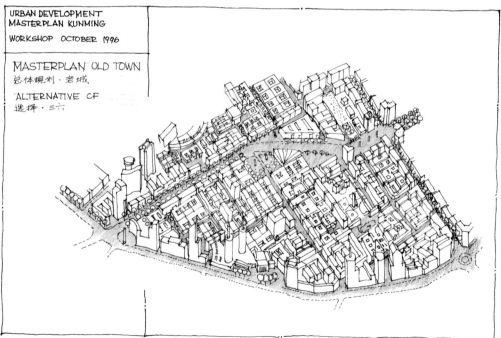

URBAN DEVELOPMENT
MASTERPLAN KUNMING
WORKSHOP OCTOBER 1996

MASTERPLAN OLD TOWN
总体规划·老城
ALTERNATIVE CF
选择·三六

Alternative concepts for the development of the historic town, based on the polarities of Growth versus Tradition and Global versus Local. 关于旧城开发工作的不同方案。这些方案均以 "发展" 与 "传统" 的矛盾和 "全球化" 与 "本地化" 的矛盾为出发点。

51

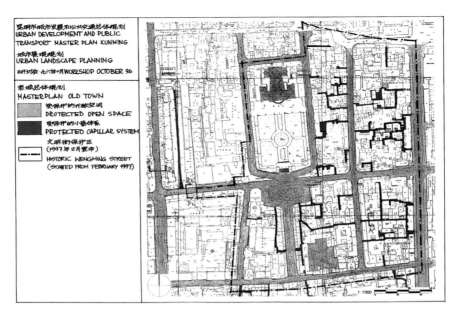

Public open space.　公共开敞空间。

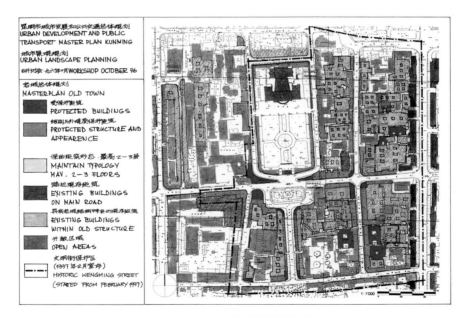

Inventory of building stock.　对建筑结构的调查。

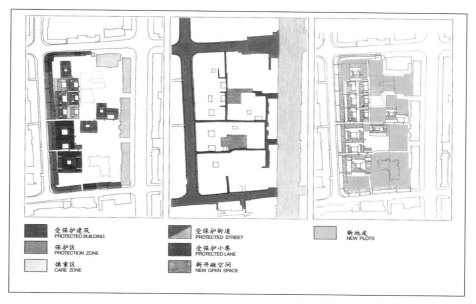

The concept for dealing with the historic town includes four stages: The urban open space must remain unchanged (dark red). The structure of traditional buildings (façades, roofs, fire walls) must be retained, especially in peripheral areas (orange). New buildings must be subordinate, in appearance and scale, to existing structures (yellow). Unique historic buildings will be protected individually. 对旧城的处理方案分为四个阶段：城市开敞空间不得进行任何改变（深红色）；传统建筑的结构（立面、屋顶和界墙）必须保留下来，尤其是在临街处（橙黄色）；与现有建筑相比，新建筑在外观和规模上都必须处于次要地位（黄色）；对独特的历史建筑应分别采取保护措施。

notes for the shaping of the modern city. The first studies on how to deal with the old city of Kunming were triggered by the construction of Renming Road, through the centre of the still very much untouched arrangement of the historic city.

At our first workshop in Kunming we were confronted with this basic conflict, found in all urban societies. How much innovation must be made possible to accommodate new needs and values? How much of the existing building stock must be preserved for the city to keep its identity and to prevent its inhabitants from becoming homeless?

当我们在昆明召开第一轮工作讨论会时，我们就遇到了每个城市社会都会面临的基本矛盾：要建设多少新东西，才能满足人们的新需求和新价值观？要保留多少现存的东西，才能使城市保持它的特色、使居民仍有一种归属感？

我们在工作讨论会中，通过一系列研究，为决定如何处理昆明旧城打下了基础。
首先，我们用草图勾画出不同的旧城处理策略将会对城市空间带来的影响；
其次，我们制订了贯彻旧城保护策略所需要的方案和工具；
最后，我们又把现存历史性建筑的开

发潜力汇编成书面资料。这项工作尤其重要，因为人们当时似乎并不相信现存建筑仍可发挥作用。

最为关键的一点就是，这些基本工作并不是由外国专家单独完成的，而是双方通过合作取得的成果。

新市区的建设

在后来举办的一次工作讨论会上，主要课题已不再是如何延续城市的历史，

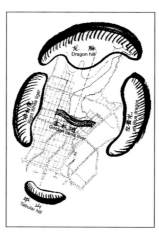

The *feng shui* interpretation of the area of the new North Town. 在北市区新城运用了风水原理。

而是如何提高新市区的质量。昆明市人口增长极为迅速，为适应这一发展，昆明市决定向北部进行大规模扩建。当时规定市区北部的整个河谷平原地带都可用于开发建设。这片长约二十公里、宽约八公里的地区，除了边缘地带以外几乎尚未进行任何开发。它建成昆明北市区后，将容纳大约五十万人居住和工作。

昆明市规划院一位女士对北市区进行了规划后，我们应邀就这个规划提出我们的看法和意见。当我询问都有哪些规划内容已经确定下来、不能

Several different starting points for decision-making were developed at our workshop.

– First, alternative scenarios were sketched out to show the spatial effects of the different strategies.
– Then, concepts and instruments were presented which could help in securing a protective strategy.
– Finally, the potential of the existing historic buildings was recorded. This was important, because evidently trust in the usefulness of the existing building stock had been lost. It was of crucial importance that this basic groundwork was not done by foreign experts, but was the product of joint work.

Building a new city

At a later workshop, the search for the meaning of the continuity of the city was no longer in the foreground; it was replaced by a search for quality in building a new urban quarter. The city was to be extended to the north, on a large scale, to deal with the rapid increase in Kunming's population. The entire valley floor was set aside, approximately 20 km long and 8 km wide, and until today, only populated along the periphery. A new city area for approximately 500 000 people to live and work in was to be created.

An employee of the urban planning department had designed a plan for the area. We were invited to reflect upon the proposed concept. My question about previously laid down policies was answered, much to my surprise, this way: apart from the motorway, only the *feng-shui* axis, leading from a hill to the north into built-up Kunming, was considered relevant. Each plan was based on a set of goals. These goals are often immanently present, without having been articulated. Single goals then receive a lot of attention in the political and cultural situation at that time because they are new or because they have a specific topicality.

再变更时，回答令我十分惊讶：除了一条高速公路以外，只有一条风水轴线不能变动。这条轴线从北部丘陵地带向南延伸至目前的昆明市区。
每一个规划都是为实现一组目标而制订的。这些目标通常并没有明文记录下来，但它们却是内在固有的。在现实的政治和文化环境中，有些目标受到高度重视，因为它们代表着新潮流，

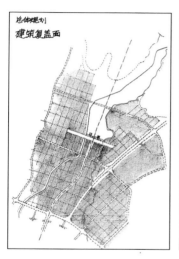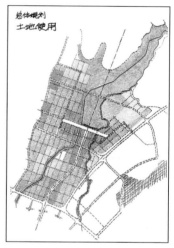

Master Plan for the new North Town:—building area—main open space— comprehensive master plan. 北市区新城的总体规划： － 建设区 － 主要开敞空间 － 综合性总体规划。

With us there were three key concepts: sustainable development, mobility, and identity.

Again, the principle behind the design of the old town was important to us. Every concept and each plan must be anchored in a higher level and be tested at a lower level.
The theme of sustainable development and mobility changed the original plan considerably. To support the development of a functional public transportation concept, an eastern and a western axis of development was proposed,

或者它们对当前情况有着特别重要的意义。
在我们的研究工作中，有三大概念尤为重要："可持续发展"、"人与物的流动"和"鲜明个性"。我们在这项研究上所遵循的基本原则，和在旧城规划上采用的原则是一样的：每一个方案、每一个规划都应在较高的层次上确定下来，并在较低的层次上进行实验。
由于提出了"可持续发展"和"人与物的流动"这两大课题，就必须对原来的北市区规划进行相当大的更

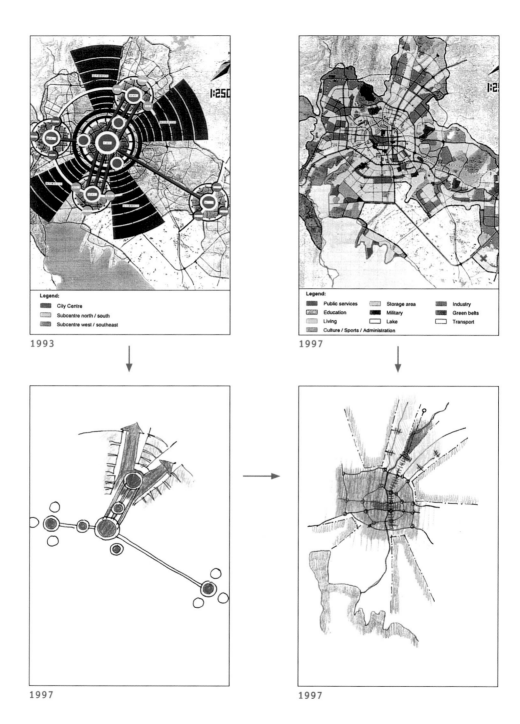

Legend:
- City Centre
- Subcentre north / south
- Subcentre west / southeast

1993

Legend:
- Public services
- Education
- Living
- Culture / Sports / Administration
- Storage area
- Military
- Lake
- Industry
- Green belts
- Transport

1997

1997

1997

Evolution of the plans for the new North Town of the Kunming Urban Planning and Design Institute (above) through successive workshops (below).

56

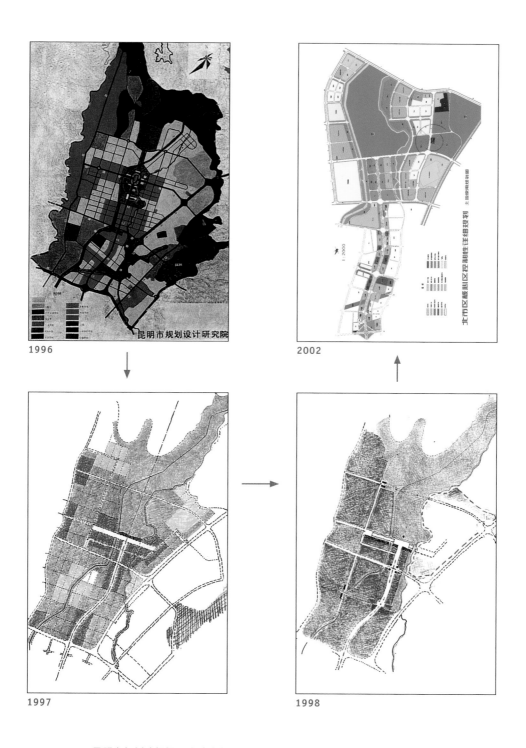

1996

昆明市规划设计研究院

2002

1997

1998

昆明市规划院根据工作讨论会的研究成果，对北市区的规划不断进行了调整。

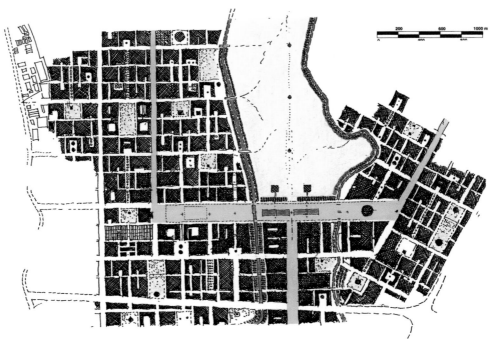

Topographic view of the central area as a guideline for urban design rules. 中心区地形图是进行城市设计的基本依据。

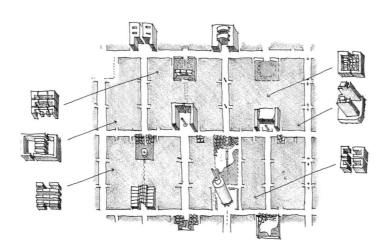

An attempt to develop a grid for structuring the new town on the basis of the *feng shui* concept. 尝试运用风水原理设计新城的布局网格。

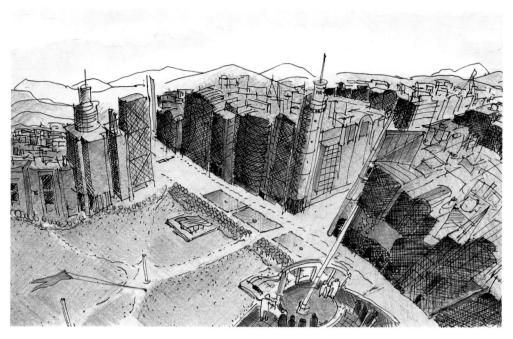

Perspective showing the north end of
Beijing Road. 北京路北端透视图。

instead of a central new focus on building
development. This permitted a more attractive public transportation system and meant
that a green belt could be drawn far into the
area from the north. At the same time, this
scheme would facilitate harmonious growth
in economically feasible steps.

We have placed much importance on verbal
communication for crossing the boundaries
between different languages. Professor Chen
Zhao, an architect from Nanjing who had
worked for several years at the Swiss Federal Institute of Technology in Zurich, ac-
companied us through all the workshops.
His presence assured us that the transla-
tions were correct, not only in words but
also in meaning. However, the drawn image

改。为了便于实现高效公共交通，
我们建议放弃原来规划里的单一市
区中心，而是建设东西两条发展轴
线。这样不仅有助于实现便捷的公共
交通体系，而且能开辟一片从北部一
直向南延伸到北市区核心的绿化带。
如果采用这种方式，还能做到在经
济上量力而行、逐步进行开发建设。

由于双方语言不同，我们在合作中就
更加重视口语交流的质量。来自南京
的赵辰教授参加了所有的工作讨论会，
他是一位建筑师，曾在位于瑞士苏
黎世的瑞士联邦工业大学工作过数
年。有他参加工作讨论会，就保证不
但字面意思，而且内容上的真正含
义也都能准确翻译给对方。尽管如
此，中瑞双方还是主要靠图片进行交

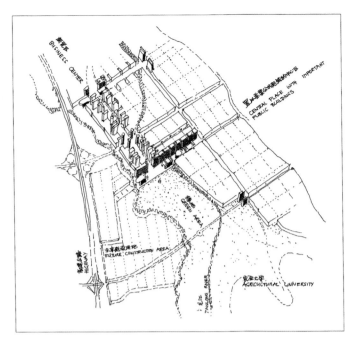

The transition from the central business axis into the landscape
park is defined with a public square. 公共广场成为中心商业区轴
线与公园之间的过渡。

流。所有的设计方案，包括北市区的
大型发展前景，都绘制成了三维立体
图。尤其是建筑类型方案和城市空
间方案，更是利用立体图进行了显
示。我们还和昆明的朋友们共同探
索如何以中国传统的城市设计为基
础，实现错落有致的街区布局，以
避免产生在发展过快的现代城市中
常见的单调感和市民的无归属感。

was always the central instrument of communication. All concepts, including the large-
scale vision of the Northern City, were drawn
three-dimensionally. This was employed especially for the detailed development of
the concept regarding typology and urban
spaces. Jointly, with our friends from Kunming, we searched for possibilities based on
traditional Chinese urban design, in order to
find, at a local level, varied urban patterns
and thereby avoid the dangers of monotony
and homelessness, often found in modern
cities that grow too rapidly.

WANG XUEHAI   王学海

Good Design is Rooted in Cultural Exchange 良好的设计来自文化交流

Different cultural backgrounds often lead to different ways of thinking and working. The experts from Zurich are from a western culture, while the planners from Kunming grew up in an eastern culture. Co-operation between them is fuelled by energy and friendship, but also enlivened by differences in outlook.

The initial phase of the co-operation

When the joint urban planning project began in 1996, the city of Kunming was one vast building site. Due to conflicting interests, we at the urban planning department were regrettably forced to witness the results of insufficient protection of public open spaces, natural landscape areas and, above all, the historic urban scenery. So the experts from Zurich were our big hope, as the opinion of urban planners from developed countries was rated highly in China.

We agreed with Carl Fingerhuth to work jointly in the areas of 'design of new neighbourhoods' and 'redesign of the city centre'. Time pressure caused us to concentrate primarily on urban design, basic principles of urban scenery, the urban fabric of the city, and principles of transportation management.

不同的文化背景通常产生不同的思维和行动方式。当来自西方文化的瑞士苏黎世专家与东方文化熏陶下的中国昆明规划师共同工作时，这个合作过程充满了激情和友谊，也不断地出现矛盾和分歧。

合作的初期

双方在城市规划方面的合作从1996年开始，当时的昆明就象一个大工地。由于各方利益的冲突，城市规划经常是让步多的一方，在保障公共绿地及活动空间、保护城市自然景观和历史景观上，尤其是在旧城保护的问题上，我们节节败退。因此，我们对苏黎世专家的参与抱了比较大的希望，这些城市规划专家毕竟来自发达国家，他们的意见将得到更多的重视。

我们与卡尔·芬格胡特先生商定，在"城市新区建设"和"城市中心区改造"这两个课题上展开合作。鉴于时间的限制，合作主要在城市设计上开展，以提供进一步深化工作的城市景观控制原则、规划结构及交通组织原则。
我当时只不过希望合作能对我们的眼前工作有所帮助。但接下来的合作所造成的深远影响，远远超出了我的想象。

61

Capillary lane
细密的街巷体系

Scale of public space.
公共空间的尺度。

Market road 市场道路

Market road 市场道路

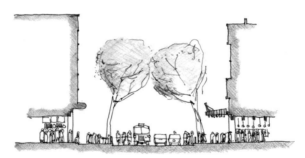

Zhengyi Road, central old town axis from the seventies
正义路曾是七十年代的旧城中轴线

Dongfeng Road 东风路

Initially, I was merely hoping that the co-operation would support our work in progress. In fact, the effects went far beyond anything I could have imagined.

When the experts from Zurich visited Kunming, they were interested in the local situation and Chinese culture right from the start. (On a later visit to the home of Carl Fingerhuth, I saw that he had many books about China.) They tried hard to understand this other culture; however, misunderstandings sometimes occurred. For example, *feng shui* encompasses basic ideas on the construction of houses and graves of the Chinese, but lacks scientific and systematic analysis. Modern China has not preserved all traditions; only the rational and scientific is to be kept.

The Kunming side was also strongly influenced by the co-operation. The careful, conscientious way in which the Zurich experts worked, as well as their respect for Chinese culture and their tireless dedication to the conservation of the historic town, moved us deeply. The Kunming experts participated with ever-increasing determination and maintained a positive attitude towards the joint project.

Design of the city centre

When the experts from Zurich presented the design concept for the city centre, I was impressed by the new opportunities. Urban traditions were safeguarded and footpath networks and pedestrian areas created. These ideas far exceeded our former designs. Everyone at our joint workshop was in favour of the concept.

An important topic of the concept was the analysis of open space in the city, especially the road spaces. The conservation of the historic town was also dealt with at a high-

当苏黎世专家小组到达昆明时，他们首先重视的是对昆明具体情况的熟悉和对中国文化的了解。（我后来到过卡尔家，看到他的书柜中有大量关于中国的书籍）。尽管他们努力尝试着了解不同的文化，仍难免产生一些误解。比如，风水学是基于中国民间建宅选墓的朴素思想而来，缺少科学系统的研究体系，而现代的中国并没有把所有传统都继承下来，实际上只有合理的、科学的才能保留。

昆明方面在合作中也受到了很大的影响。除了苏黎世专家严谨认真的工作态度外，他们对中国传统文化的尊重和对昆明老城保护的执着也深深地感动了我们。昆明专家更加坚定了决心，以积极的态度投入到合作工作中。

城市中心区城市设计

当我第一次看到苏黎世专家小组提出的昆明城市中心区城市设计方案时，有一种耳目一新的感觉。城市传统列入了严格的保护，并建议开辟城市步行体系以及步行区。这些设计突破了我们原有的任何一次规划。这个方案在合作小组讨论时，得到了大家的认同赞许。

城市空间环境的分析是本次城市设计的一个重要内容，街道的空间感受尤其受到重视。旧城保护也提高到了很高的层次。苏黎世专家使用的街巷空间与建筑实体空间别离分析，与中国传统文化风水中的阴阳理论惊人地相似。

在结合实施难度的方案确定中，卡尔·芬格胡特先生带领下的苏黎世专家组，采用了一种类似于排除法的图表分析方法。这种方法与中国传统中的"中庸"学说极为相似，即列出一个最保守的和一个最激进的方案，再在它们之间取一个折衷方案。

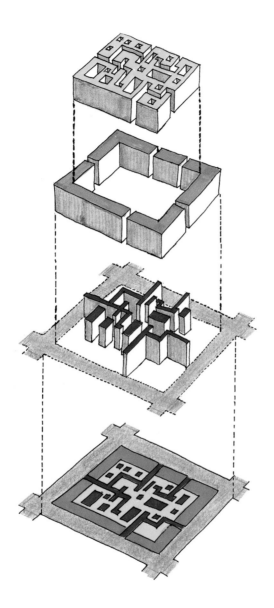

An old town block is a complex
system of built-up and open spaces.
旧城内的街区是由建筑和开敞空间组
成的一个复杂体系。

er level. One method employed by the Zurich experts was an analysis of the inter-relationship between road spaces and the spaces of individual buildings. This is surprisingly similar to the yin-yang theory in *feng shui*.

Several concepts were analysed by Carl Fingerhuth and his team regarding implementation of the plan. An extremely conservative concept and a very progressive one were presented, finally leading to an agreement on a compromise. This method is similar to the 'teaching of the middle course' in Chinese tradition.

The main disagreement related to the feasibility of the concept. Some of the ideas were difficult to implement, but both partners were in favour of pursuing the realisation of the concept and we applied for approval of this ideal concept.

Implementation and the far-reaching consequences

So far, the schemes implemented in the city centre and the North City have produced good results. A concept for the conservation area in the historic town was set out; pedestrian zones were implemented in stages. Links from public transportation to pedestrian areas were put into place successfully. The planning concept for the North City was approved and became the legal basis for implementation. Today, the southern part of the North City is largely built according to that concept, while the development zones in the northern part are strictly limited, also in keeping with the concept.

The far-reaching consequences of this co-operative effort go beyond the implementation of the project. First, the opinions of the Chinese and Swiss experts were both strongly affected—this is the most important result of the joint work. Both partners understand and respect the other's culture. The experts from Zurich brought modern ideas of urban planning, which were systematically integrated into the work of the Kunming planners who have been and will be implementing them. The technical co-operation has not only supported the urban planning of Kunming, but has also made the design work and its implementation more transparent: urban planners now take more notice of social aspects such as the economy and community life. In April 2000, the city of Kunming built a model to illustrate the conservation concept for the historic town. The city asked its inhabitants for feedback on the conservation concept—95 per cent of 10 000 responses were in favour of protection. It has now become a necessity to invite the public to participate in important urban planning decisions.

No two cities are alike. If Zurich had applied its experience unaltered to Kunming, the project would have failed. Active cultural exchange between the Zurich experts and the urban planners from Kunming, the Swiss experts' profound understanding of the

双方在城市设计上的主要分歧在于实施上的可能性。一些设想的实施难度较大。但双方都认为应当实施这个方案，因此，此次城市设计的理想方案上报。

实施效果与深远影响

从已经实施的效果来看，城市中心区城市设计与北市新区城市设计的实施效果很好。城市中心区已划定了文明街历史街区保护范围并制订了保护规划，城市步行区已按规划逐步实施，城市公共交通与步行街区的良好结合已被认可。城市北市新区规划已通过了审批，成为规划实施的法律依据。现在北市区的南部已大部分按规划实施，而北部的建设用地也已按规划进行了严格控制。

实施效果固然良好，而此次合作产生的深远影响则更为巨大。首先，合作中带来的最重要影响是对中瑞双方专家思想的影响，对不同文化的理解和尊重得到了加强。苏黎世专家带来的先进的城市设计思想被昆明市规划师系统地接受，今后将得到进一步实施。双方技术上的合作除了推进昆明的城市规划与设计之外，也使昆明的规划制订和实施更加开放，更多的社会因素被城市规划所重视，如城市规划对城市经济、社会的改善等。2000年4月，昆明市政府将文明街区的保护规划制作成模型，向广大市民征求意见。从回收的一万余件意见书中看，赞成保护的意见达到了95%。公众参与城市规划这一方法已经成为我们推行重要城市规划的一个必须步骤。

没有一个城市是另一个城市的翻版。如果苏黎世把它的经验照搬到昆明，项目将会失败。苏黎世专家与昆明城市规划师在文化方面的积极交流，苏黎世专家对中国文化的深入理解和对昆明传统的尊重，以及昆明城市规划师对苏黎世先进经验的积极吸收，是双方合作成功的坚实基础，因为，良好的城市设计来自文化的积极交流！

Chinese culture, their respect for the traditions of Kunming, and finally the active absorption of the modern know-how from Zurich by the Kunming urban planners, all formed a solid foundation for successful cooperation—because good urban design is based on active cultural exchange!

Development North Town, 2002.　北市区的开发，2002年。

WERNER STUTZ　威尔纳·施图茨

Conservation of Historic Monuments　保护历史建筑

Up until a few years ago, Kunming had a large, homogeneous and fascinating historic town. Then significant areas were sacrificed for the modernisation of the city. It was mostly the timber houses that were demolished without being replaced; in some places attempts were made to recreate the atmosphere of the historic town.

The design workshops in 1997 and 1998 created the preconditions for political decision making, on a methodological level and on a concrete level, to place the most important parts of the historic town under protection, in the Wen Ming Protection Area (1998). It then became of the utmost importance to assist the city authorities of Kunming in the implementation of the plan for the conservation areas. A period of intense cooperation between those responsible in the city of Kunming and experts from the city of Zurich began.

Theory and Practice

First, the methodology had to be developed for compiling inventories, that is, for the systematic recording and evaluation of the existing historic building stock that merited protection. Also, a survey of the street façades needed to be made, to catalogue materials and assess their state of repair.

To establish the necessary expert knowledge, an in-depth exchange of experience

直至数年前，昆明还拥有风格统一、引人入胜的大面积旧城。后来，旧城的绝大部分都成了城市现代化改造的牺牲品。其中被拆掉而又没有重建的主要是木结构房屋。在有些地方，也进行了恢复旧城原有氛围的尝试。

Corner house in the Wen Ming Protection Area.　受保护的文明街历史街区内一座位于街角处的房屋。

1997年和1998年举办的工作讨论会为市政府的决策打下了基础。工作讨论会研究了保护旧城最重要片区（文明街片区）的工作方法和工作内容，使

67

The centre of the Wen Ming Protection Area.
受保护的文明街历史街区的中心地带。

传统建筑 traditional building

新建筑 new building

露天空间 open-air space

老旧庭院 historical court

Example of a façade survey sheet: timber house.
一份房屋立面调查表: 木结构房屋。

MATERIAL 建筑材料

Wood 木材

plasterwork 灰泥

coating 涂料

ARCHITECTURAL CONDITION OF FAÇADE 立面建筑状况

unspoilt, original quality 木遭破坏，保持原有

unspoilt, original quality, No 32 change and interference 木遭破坏，保持原有质量，第 32 号已改

68

took place. Two employees of the Kunming Urban Planning and Design Institute visited Zurich for practical training. They were taught methods of making inventories, the practice of conservation of historic monuments, administrative procedures, and legal instruments.

The second step was a six-day seminar, in which urban planners and architects of the Kunming Urban Planning and Design Institute, one employee of the city museum, and students from Yunnan Polytechnic University, as well as several employees of the Zurich conservation department, participated. The recording, evaluation and documentation of existing building stock was taught and trained in theory and practice: façade inventory, urban area analysis (old and new buildings, open space and courtyards), analysis of individual houses, utilisation analysis, and a survey of structural damage.

Out of this co-operative process, a manual was compiled which laid out the methodological guidelines and practical foundations of conservation work.

Also of great importance was the creation of a new department within the Kunming local authority in the year 2000. The Kunming Historical Street Block and Building Protection Office is now the institution responsible for implementing protection and restoration work.

Subsequently the joint conservation efforts were expanded to other old built-up areas that were not part of the protected historic town. This work was accepted by the city of Kunming and integrated into the ongoing planning process and negotiations with investors and developers.

这个片区于1997年成为受保护的"文明街历史街区"。从那时起，协助昆明市有关部门在保护区内实施保护措施，就成了我们最重要的任务。于是，昆明市和苏黎世市的负责人员展开了密切合作。

理论与实践

当时的首要任务是研究用什么样的方法展开现状调查工作，以便系统地记录并评估应受保护的历史建筑。同时还应调查沿街房屋立面的建材和需要采取的维修措施。

为使有关人员汲取必要的专业知识，双方深入交流了专业经验。昆明市规划院的两位工作人员到苏黎世接受了实践培训。他们学习了进行现状调查的工作方法、保护历史建筑的实践、管理程序以及法律工具。

之后，双方举办了为期六天的讲座，参加者包括昆明市规划院的城市规划师和建筑师、市博物馆的一位工作人员、云南工业大学的学生们和苏黎世文物局的数位专家。在这次讲座中，传授了关于现存房屋的调查、评估和资料编写工作的理论与实践，如房屋立面调查、片区分析（新旧建筑、开敞空间及院落）、房屋个例分析、使用功能分析及房屋结构受损情况调查等。

在上述合作过程中还编订了一份工作手册，介绍了文物保护工作的基本方法和实践。

此外，还有一项非常重要的工作，就是昆明市规划局在2000年设立了一个新的下属机构"昆明历史街区与建筑保护办公室"。现在，这个办公室负责实施保护及维修工作。

随后，双方在文物保护方面的合作又扩大到了文明街历史街区以外的其它旧城地区。昆明市对这一工作给予了

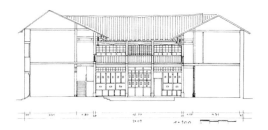

I-I 剖面 Section 1:100

Section through historic town houses, a task for building research.
一座旧城传统房屋的剖面图，对这座房屋应进行建筑研究。

肯定，并把它纳入了今后的规划工作和与房地产投资商的谈判工作中。

金兰茶苑

为了尝试文物保护的理论和实践，昆明选择了老城内的一座传统宅院作为样板项目，实际运用了文物保护工作程序并记录成册。现在，这座宅院的业主已经对它进行了维修保护。

The Jin Lan Tea House

In order to test theory and practice, a historic courtyard house in the old town was used as an example. The pilot conservation procedure was rehearsed and then documented in a brochure. Meanwhile, this house has been refurbished by its owner.

Jin Lan Tea House, 1st Floor, after renovation.
维修后的金兰茶苑二楼。

GAO XUEMEI 高雪梅

The Concept of Heritage Preservation 文物保护方案

Kunming is one of the most historic cities in China. In the 1996 co-operative project between Kunming and Zurich, the historic town and building preservation became an important concept to be researched and discussed. This has resulted in significant improvements for Kunming.

The main areas of co-operation included three aspects: planning for the preservation of the built heritage of the city, promoting the renovation and renewal of the old city, and preservation management of the old city. After six years of co-operation with Zurich, we have gained much experience, not only in professional areas, but also the area of management. In urban planning, we finally accepted the concept of the preservation of old towns or streets. The local governors updated their thoughts by consulting the Zurich experts, and gained experience by visiting the old town of Zurich. The professional people enhanced their skills by participating in the co-operation project, and through training in Zurich.

昆明是中国的历史名城之一。1996年，历史街区与建筑的保护工作，成为昆明与苏黎世合作项目中一个倍受关注

Renovation of a historic town house.
维修旧城内的一座传统房屋。

的重要课题。这项合作为昆明带来了巨大的帮助。

合作的主要内容包括三个方面，即制订昆明市建筑遗产保护规划、推动旧城维修及更新工作、加强对旧城保护工作的管理。经过与苏黎世的六年合作，我们无论是在专业领域还是在管理方面都汲取了很多经验。在城市规划方面，历史片区与街道保护方案最终被认可；昆明的领导们与苏黎世专家展开了交流并考察了苏黎世的旧城，

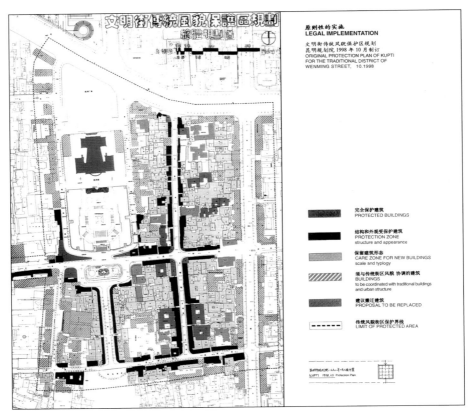

文明街传统风貌保护区规划
总体规划图

原则性的实施
LEGAL IMPLEMENTATION
文明街传统风貌保护区规划
昆明规划院 1998 年 10 月制订
ORIGINAL PROTECTION PLAN OF KUPTI
FOR THE TRADITIONAL DISTRICT OF
WENMING STREET, 10.1998

完全保护建筑
PROTECTED BUILDINGS

结构和外观受保护建筑
PROTECTION ZONE
structure and appearance

保留建筑形态
CARE ZONE FOR NEW BUILDINGS
scale and typlogy

须与传统街区风貌 协调的建筑
BUILDINGS
to be coordinated with traditional buildings
and urban structure

建议置迁建筑
PROPOSAL TO BE REPLACED

传统风貌街区保护界线
LIMIT OF PROTECTED AREA

昆明市规划院·一九·年·10·总体方案
KUPTI 1998.10. Protection Plan

Protection plan adopted by the Kunming government
in 1997. 昆明市政府于1997年决定的保护规划。

从而改变了他们原来的看法；昆明的专业人员通过参加合作项目以及到苏黎世接受培训，提高了他们的专业水平。

在将近六年的时间里，合作取得了下列丰硕成果：

文明街区保护规划最终获得了政府批准；维修及更新工作的样板项目"金兰茶苑"荣获"联合国教科文组织亚太地区文化遗产保护奖"；昆明设立了"昆明历史街区与建筑保护办公室"负责昆明历史片区及街道的管理。

Within about six years, the co-operation has led to many achievements:

The preservation plan for the Wen Ming district finally received approval from the government; the pilot renovation and renewal project—the Jin Lan Tea House—received the UNESCO Asia-Pacific Heritage Award; and the Kunming Historic Town Preservation Office, which is responsible for the Kunming historic area and street management, was established.

As a professional person who participated in the whole process of the old town preservation co-operation project, I feel that the co-operation between Kunming and Zurich has successfully promoted the theory and practice of urban planning and management in Kunming. Now the concept of heritage preservation has been implanted into everyone's minds. Every city should have its own unique characteristics and identity. The preservation benefits both society and economic development. We have not only added to the prosperity of our city, but have also preserved a piece of the history of our city. Although there is a long hard road ahead, we can see a bright future. Meanwhile, we should continue to search for the best ways for Chinese old town heritage preservation to take place.

作为一名自始至终参加旧城保护合作项目的专业人员，我感到昆明与苏黎世的合作成功地加强了昆明城市规划与管理的意识和能力。现在，文物保护意识已经深入人心。每座城市都应有它独特的个性和特色，文物保护工作对社会和经济发展都十分有益。我们不但应促进城市的经济繁荣，而且应保护我们城市的历史。虽然任重道远，我们已看到了光明的未来。现在，我们应继续努力寻求一条适合中国国情的正确道路，保护珍贵的历史名城遗产。

Joiners and carpenters are wanted.　木工非常抢手。

The development 开发

应尊重独特的滇池盆地，

the landscape,　景观,

agriculture 农业

and rural life, 和乡村生活,

rediscovering the spirit　恢复当地的

of the site.　原有风貌。

e road system, but the 　并非公路体系，

existing rail tracks, w

e the backbone 而是现有的铁路轨道

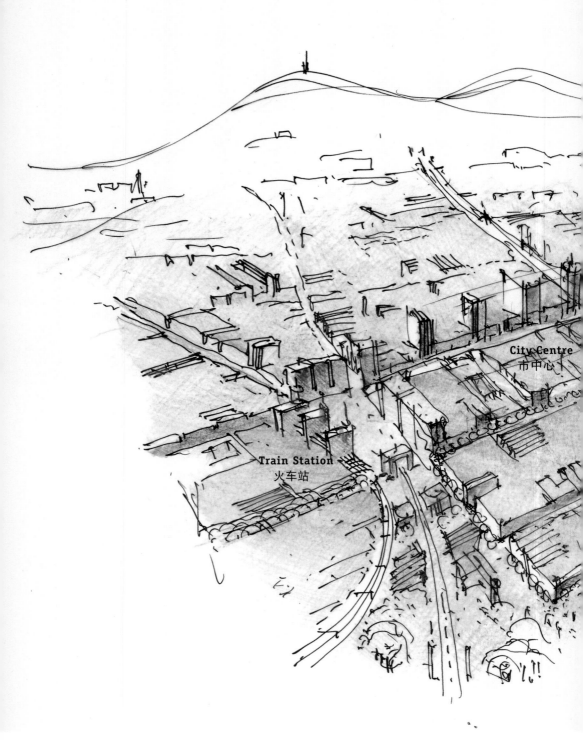

Train Station
火车站

City Centre
市中心

of the new satellite town network. 将

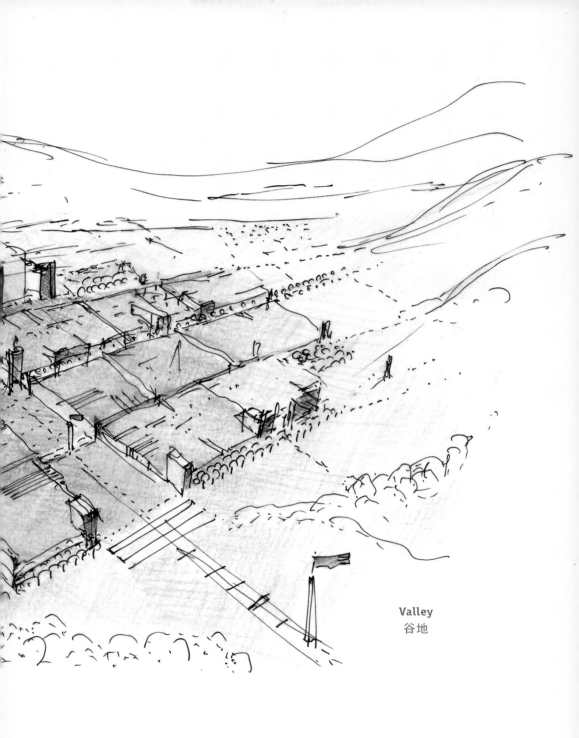

Valley
谷地

新卫星城网络的交通骨干。

Centre and periphery.　中心与边缘地带。

MATTHIAS WEHRLIN　玛提亚斯·魏尔林

Urban Design within the Greater Kunming Region
大昆明区的城市设计

Spring City

I am overwhelmed each time the airplane turns into the wide expanse of the Kunming area to begin its landing approach. On the long flight from Beijing or Shanghai, over the jagged landscape of central China, the endless sequences of mountains and hills, steep slopes and valleys cut by erosion, interrupted by only a few plateaus, it becomes apparent that this most densely populated country of the world has only 7 per cent of productive agricultural land to feed its people from. On the much shorter flight from Bangkok over impenetrable jungle, cut by the brown waters of the Mekong River and over the Black and Red Rivers in the borderlands of northern Burma, Thailand and Laos, and over Yunnan's southernmost district, Xishuangbanna, the strategic location of Kunming in the far south of China becomes clear.

On the last part of the approach to landing in Kunming one sees not only uninhabited, wooded hills, or clay pits, rice fields and small settlements; there are also newly built roads, huge construction sites, and recently completed housing areas outside the city, showing how far urban development has penetrated into the region. Shortly before touch-down, a silhouette dominated by

春城

每次乘飞机到昆明，当飞机驶近昆明地区上空准备降落的时候，我总是感到心潮澎湃，不能自已。从北京或者上海飞往昆明，一路上只望得见蜿蜒起伏的中华大地：连绵群山似乎看不到头，崇山峻岭被岁月雕刻出鲜明棱角，只有小小的高原和平原点缀其间。看到这幅景象，就不难理解这个人口数量居世界之最的国家，为什么只能靠世界上百分之七的耕地面积解决人民的吃饭问题。如果从曼谷飞往昆明，则要飞越澜沧江、黑河、红河等名川大河，以及缅甸、泰国和老挝三国交界处极少人行的莽莽丛林，还要经过云南省最南端的西双版纳自治州。飞机抵达昆明时，就可以明显看出昆明在中国南部的地理位置有多么重要了。

在飞机降落前的最后一段飞行中，映入眼帘的不但有森林茂密的丘陵、土石裸露的山丘、陶土开采工地、稻田和小村镇；新修的道路、大型建筑工地和雨后春笋般新建的小区也同样吸引着我们的目光，并清清楚楚地告诉我们，昆明的开发建设活动早已深入了整个大昆明地区。在飞机即将着陆前的最后一刻，由高楼大厦勾画出的城市风景在窗外飞逝而过，它们体现了这座城市飞快的发展节奏。在西山的衬托下，一座现代化城市展现在人们的眼前。如果是夜间抵达昆明，市区华灯灿烂，璀璨动人。而就在几年前，夜晚的昆明还笼罩在黑暗的夜色之中。

昆明市的建设面积，早已超出了历史上的市区范围。这座享有"春城"[1]美誉的历史名城，正处于迅猛发展和深刻变革之中。市政府的有关部门也已意识到了这一点[2]。

城市的尺度和个性

直到1945年以前，昆明还拥有完整的城墙和少量的郊区。城内的院落和店铺密集如织，大街、道路和狭窄的小巷纵横其间。随着工业化水平的提高和1979年左右开始实行的改革开放政策，昆明在过去二十多年中取得了跳跃式的发展。市区面积成倍扩大，呈现出新的尺度。

1970年，昆明老城的传统中轴线——正义路得到了重修和拓宽。昆明市现在的中轴线则是北京路，它从市区南部的昆明火车站一直通向北部很远的地带。一环路多年以来就早已成为城市格局的一部分。二环路是无交叉路口的高架路，它把许多重要的出入道路连接起来，并使昆明与呈放射状通向各地的快速路连通。现在已经可以看出三环路的雏形，它距市区较远，将在北、东、南三面环绕昆明市。在三环路的交叉路口附近，轰轰烈烈的开发建设活动已经展开了。至少在这里就应实施强有力的区域城市发展布局战略，这一战略将与景观元素相协调，并以高效快速市郊铁路体系为依托。

省会城市昆明市的开发建设区不可能无限扩大，它的自然边界就是西部陡峭的西山和东部及北部的山丘。按照区域发展方案，从昆明主城向外有计划地开辟辐射状的、长度均在30至

the high-rise buildings of this rapidly growing town flows past the cabin window. The skyline of a modern city unfolds before the backdrop of the West Mountains. At every new landing, brightly lit scenery replaces what was enveloped in darkness only a few years back.

Urban development spills over the historic town boundary. 'Spring City',[1] rich in tradition, is in a phase of rapid growth and dramatic change. This was also recognised by the municipal authorities.[2]

Scale and Identity

Until 1945, Kunming was hemmed in by town walls, with only a few early suburbs. A network of streets, paths and passages structured the dense carpet of courtyard houses and market houses. Industrialisation and the opening of the economy in 1979 led to spasmodic growth over the past two decades. The area covered by the town has multiplied, and a new scale has been introduced.

In 1970, Zhengyi Road, the historic axis of the old town, was repaired and widened. The central axis of today's town is Beijing Road, which will lead from the main railway station in the south to far in the north. The first ring road has been part of the urban fabric for years. The second ring, a intersection-free road at an elevated level, links the important access roads with one another and connects Kunming to high-capacity roads leading radially away from the city. Now, the outlines of a third ring road can be detected a long way from the city; it will first enclose Kunming on the north, east and south. Already the development of radially spreading settlements at the junctions of this ring has begun. Here, at last, the strategy of a strong, regional urban development pattern aligned with landscape elements has been applied, including access points to an efficient Rapid Suburban Railway network.

The growth of settlements comes up against natural boundaries: the steep flanks of the West Mountains and the hills to the north and east of the capital of the province. The concept of structured, radial axes of development, each approximately 30–40 km in length, establishes an alternative to peripheral sprawl.

40公里左右的发展轴线，比目前那种"摊大饼式"的建设方式要好得多：

－ 这些区域发展轴线与云南省确定的经济发展轴线基本一致。

－ 高效交通体系已经建设完成，或正在规划、建设之中。大昆明地区将主要依靠既有铁路线建设快速市郊铁路体系，作为未来城市发展的交通骨干。沿线除已有的少量火车站外，还将新建一大批火车站。火车站周围地带将

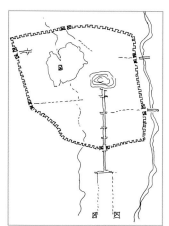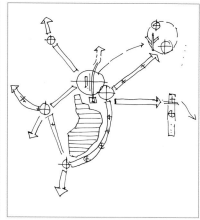

The scale and extent of the city have changed at a dramatic rate. Until the Second World War, Kunming was enclosed by town walls, with a central axis approximately 1 km in length (left). The axis of today's city between the railway station in the south and North Town measures about 10 km in length (centre). The regional urban plan (right) will have a diameter of approximately 80 km.

昆明市区的尺度和范围都发生了巨大变化。直至第二次世界大战结束之前，昆明还拥有完整的城墙和一条长约一公里的中轴线（左图）。如今，市区的新轴线从南部的火车站一直贯穿到北市区，总长度约达10公里（中图）。整个大昆明区的城镇布局（右图）半径约为80公里。

－ The regional development axes essentially follow the economic development axes defined by the Province of Yunnan.

－ Various high-capacity means of transportation already exist, are under construction, or are planned. The backbone of the urban development plan is the Rapid Suburban Railway, which can, to a large extent, be installed on existing tracks. Urban development

成为未来新城镇的中心，那里将有着最高的建设密度，呈现出一片繁华景象。除了快速市郊铁路体系以外，还将在各城镇建设公共汽车系统和自行车及步行道路网。

－ 在新的开发建设区和新卫星城镇附近，将就近开辟休闲地带。

－ 在最适于农业生产的地带，将不进行任何开发建设活动。

– 尊重当地的景观和生态。各建设区和城镇的布局，将依照当地的内在联系、自然景观、本地历史、既有建设状况和地形特点来设计。
– 在各城镇开辟为数不多的、符合当地特点的轴线，城市设计将以这些轴线为基础展开。建成区与城市公园和其它休闲地带形成对照，相互呼应。
– 由于很多地方的建筑形式都偏于重复、缺乏个性，在城市设计中就必须对道路、广场、公园及市区边界的位置和设计作出精心考虑，赋予当地明显特色，与其它城镇区别开来。

1998年至2002年期间，双方有关部门的专业人员共同召开了数次工作讨论

The Kunming — Songming axis.　昆明－嵩明轴线。

会，针对大昆明地区未来城镇的布局规划，选出一些关键课题进行了研究，并制订了具有示范意义的解决方案。

昆明－嵩明轴线

由于昆明第二国际机场计划建在嵩明县城和杨林镇附近，这两座城镇变得十分重要。新机场将建设火车站，直接与规划的快速市郊铁路体系相连。

and its centres are focussed on the locations of the railway stations, most of them new. Here the greatest building densities should be reached. The Rapid Suburban Railway will be complemented by local bus, bicycle and footpath networks.
– New development areas and satellite towns will be allocated local recreation areas.
– The best agricultural production land will not be populated.
– Landscape and ecology will be respected. The inner logic of each site will be drawn on; the landscape, local history and its remaining built landmarks, as well as the rules of topography, are constituent elements.
  – The urban design is based on a few axes precisely cut out for each site, and balances the built-up areas with urban parks or other recreational areas.
  – In view of the generally rather repetitive, anonymous architecture, the urban design seeks to provide identity and uniqueness through the layout and design of streets and squares, parks and urban borders.
  During the years 1998 to 2002, interdisciplinary workshops concerned with different key locations of the future regional urban fabric worked on sample solutions.

Kunming—Songming Axis

The small town of Songming and the village of Yanglin are of special importance because of the international airport proposed nearby. The airport can be directly linked to the proposed Rapid Suburban Railway network. Yanglin, located outside the airport's

A model satellite town on the Kunming — Songming axis leans against the sheltering hill and opens onto the valley to the south. 座落在昆明 – 嵩明轴线上的一座示范卫星城，它背靠山丘，面向南部的河谷。

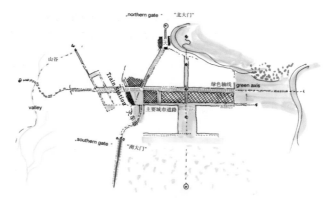

A cross-axis defines the structure of the model city. 十字形轴线确定了示范城市的总体布局。

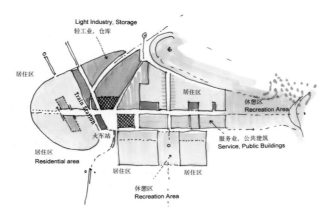

All the important service facilities are located between the parallel roads linked to the railway station. 重要的商业和公共设施都集中在通往火车站的平行道路之间。

Aerial view of Kunming East, Spring 2002. In the centre of the picture is the future railway station, where a secondary city centre will develop, linked directly to the high-tech area of Kunming East. 昆明东市区俯瞰，2002年春。照片中间是未来的火车站站址，那里将形成一个市区次中心，它直接与昆明东部的经济技术开发区相连。

杨林镇不受未来机场的噪音干扰，并将获得机场带来的巨大经济发展动力，因此，它将成为一座非常重要的卫星城。沿昆明－嵩明/杨林铁路线，将建设一批新城镇。2002年初，铁路线的设计工作已相当深入，一座卫星城已在规划之中，而第二机场的选址问题也即将最终落实。

昆明东市区和滇池东岸（至昆阳）发展轴线

昆明东南部滇池盆地一带，开发建设活动似乎没有遇到任何阻力和制约。这片地区的建设面积已达10%至20%，矿场和采石场面积大约占5%至10%。迄今为止建设面积中的70%左右占用的是肥沃良田。该地区开发方案的重点如下：
－ 在昆明东市区建设一个崭新的中心区

zone of noise impact and strengthened by its economic impulses, can develop into an important satellite town. Several towns will develop along the railway line between Kunming and Songming/Yanglin. As of early 2002, the planning of the Rapid Suburban Railway line is well advanced, a satellite town is proposed and the site of the airport is about to be decided.

Kunming East and the development axis along the eastern shore of Lake Dian

Without apparent resistance, urban development flows into the lake basin southeast of Kunming. Ten to twenty per cent of the area is built over, five to ten per cent of the area is used for extraction. Up to now, approximately 70 per cent of the settlements

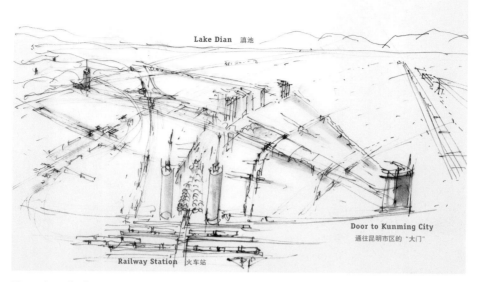

Lake Dian 滇池

Door to Kunming City
通往昆明市区的"大门"

Railway Station 火车站

The urban design concept for the development area of Kunming East proposes carefully placed landmarks as signs to facilitate orientation. The planned train station for Kunming East is in the foreground. 昆明东部开发区的城市设计方案中精心设计了一些标志性建筑，易于人们辨别方向。前景为规划的昆明东客站站址。

were put up at the expense of losing valuable agricultural land. The development concept places emphasis on the following:

- Development of a new centre including a railway station at Kunming East. Development of further local centres in relation to the remaining stations of the Rapid Suburban Railway network to follow.
- Creation of development space for logistical centres, work areas, and residential areas, and possibly a university campus.
- A system of road axes, squares, parks and landmarks should facilitate orientation and, at the same time, provide a unique urban landscape of a high spatial quality.
- Restriction of urban development in favour of valuable agricultural land, and of a development strip in the east.

和一座新火车站。围绕未来快速市郊铁路沿线的其它火车站建设更多的中心。

- 为未来的货物储运中心、工作区、居住区以至大学城预留出相应的建设空间。
- 由道路轴线、广场、公园和标志性建筑物组成的空间体系便于人们辨别方向，同时有助于形成具有高度空间质量和鲜明个性的城市空间。
- 严格控制城市发展的边界，保护优质良田，明确界定建成区的东部边界。

为了适应新的情况，昆明市有关部门在2002年开始重新规划整个昆明东市区。滇池盆地在呈贡和昆阳之间的这一段，以东面的丘陵为界。这些丘陵与滇池的距离远近不一。在丘陵与滇池之间，是土质肥沃、用作集约农业生产的一带平坦良田，它被几条横向山脉

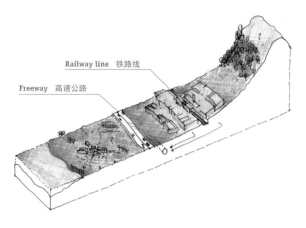

Schematic cross-section of the eastern shore of Lake Dian. The embankment
will be re-naturalised; agricultural land on the plain will be protected; the
population of the area along the railway line, river and hills will be limited
to a few towns. 滇池东岸横断面示意图。湖岸将恢复自然状态，平原上的农田将
获得保护，居民将集中在铁路沿线、河流沿岸和山脚下的少数几座城镇中居住。

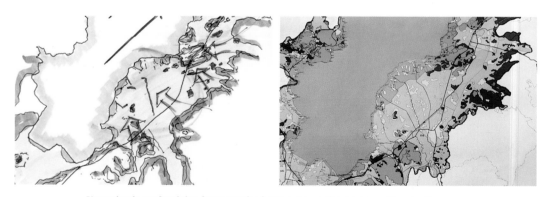

Kunming's authorities have worked out a new scheme according to the concepts of sustainable landscape development. Left sketch from the report *Lake
Dian East Shore Development,* 2001; right, layout plan, 2002. 昆明有关部
门制订了一份符合景观可持续发展原则的新规划。左图引自2001年《滇池东岸发展
报告》，右图为2002年的布局规划。

In 2002, in view of new background conditions, the authorities of the city of Kunming have begun a complete redesign of the Kunming East area.

The basin of Lake Dian, between Chenggong and Kunyang, is walled to the east by hills at varying distances from the lake. In between, along Lake Dian, lies a band of flat, fertile land under intense agricultural cultivation, subdivided by transverse ribs into single landscape rooms and river deltas opening onto Lake Dian. At the foot of the hills, small towns have developed which receive economic stimulus from the new Kunming–Yuxi motorway. The plain and delta are cultivated by people from an amorphous network of small villages. The following principles for the sustainable development of this area were laid down during two workshops in 2001:

– The paramount goal is the conservation of the landscape and respect for the natural ecology. Special attention should be paid to the local ecology. The mostly artificial lake embankments should be re-naturalised.

– Urban development will be concentrated on existing towns. The previously planned railway line will be redesigned as a Rapid Suburban Railway. The existing motorway forms the outer boundary to urban development towards Lake Dian.

The authorities have, in the meantime, worked out a landscape development plan for the Lake Dian basin. It covers 1154 sq. km, and encompasses four counties and 28 communities with a population of approximately 3 million people. This plan envisages the following cross-section at the eastern lakeshore: approximately 20 metres of wooded, re-naturalised embankment zone; followed by natural landscape; then intense agricultural use; with natural, ecological cultivation on the slopes.

分割成几个相对独立的、面向滇池的山水田园景观空间和河流三角洲。在丘陵的山脚下已有一些小城镇，新建的昆明－玉溪高速公路为这些小城镇的发展注入了巨大的经济动力。另外还有一些小居民点不规则地分布在肥沃平原和三角洲地带，居民主要从事农业。2001年，双方举办了两次工作讨论会，就这一地区的可持续发展问题制订了下列基本原则：

– 这里的最高目标是保护自然景观，尊重自然生态。尤其应重视当地的生态。应使目前的人工湖岸返回自然湖岸的状态。

– 未来的开发建设活动应集中在现已有的城镇中进行。原来已经规划了的铁路线将根据快速短途客运火车的需要重新规划。开发建设活动，最远只能到目前已建成的高速公路为止，不得蚕食滇池与高速公路之间的土地。

昆明有关部门已制订出了滇池盆地控制性规划。规划面积1154平方公里，涉4县28个乡镇，共约三百万人口。根据这份规划，滇池东岸的"横断面"将由下列部分组成：首先是宽约20米的、恢复自然状态的湖岸，这里将栽满树木，形成林带；然后是自然景观区；其后是集约农业区；在山坡上则发展自然的生态农业。

官渡

官渡古镇座落在昆明东南部的小平原上，距昆明东市区不远，它曾是历史上的一个重要渡口。应把官渡建成一处具有文化和旅游价值的名胜。官渡由四座相连的村庄组成，座落在宝象河的下游。官渡古镇目前状况不佳，令人担忧。官渡的中心矗立着著名的金刚塔，还有几座庙宇和佛塔与低矮的传统民居相映成趣。附近修有绕行道路，避免古镇受到过多交通干扰。修复一新的官渡古镇中心不但与绕行

Guandu

道路相通，还有一个集市，附近的村民也可来此赶集购货。

2000年举行的工作讨论会确定了以下规划原则：
- 停车泊位设在古镇范围以外的地点。
- 保留古镇布局模式、狭窄街巷和传统

Guandu—an old, small, former harbour on the Kunming plain—is to be developed into a focal point for culture and tourism. Guandu made up of four merged villages and situated on a small river, is in poor condition. A centrally located stupa (a round, domed, shrine), several temples, and a pagoda stand out from the traditional everyday architecture of low courtyard houses. The new centre and its market are accessible by road and function as a shopping district for the surrounding villages as well.

The following design statements were made at the workshops in 2000:
- Siting of car parks outside the historic town.
- Retaining the existing urban pattern, the system of narrow lanes, traditional courtyard houses,

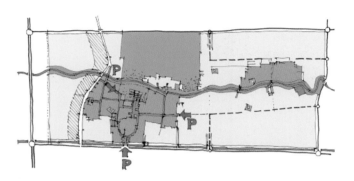

Guandu. The development of Guandu from four villages located along the small river should be retained, as well as the direct landscape link to the central temple site.
官渡。官渡由座落在宝象河边的四个村落发展而来。应保留这一格局，并保持镇中心的寺庙与自然景观之间的直接衔接。

民居，并保留镇区与绿色空间形成的鲜明对比。
- 在古镇的历史性镇中心之内和之外，都对新建建筑加以限制。
- 不仅应修复"文物"，例如金刚塔，还应恢复和维护当地民居，尤其是濒临毁坏的部分。
- 放弃修建两条新道路的计划。因为这两条道路不但会破坏当地建筑格局，还会破坏宝象河开敞空间，而宝象河则是这座古镇的"母亲河"。

上述建议大都得到了采纳。修复工程于2001年开始，总耗资约四千万人民币，其中云南省政府承担了很大一部分。

the contrast between urban and green areas.
- Limiting new buildings inside and outside the historic town centre.
- Not only 'monuments' should be renewed; reconstruction and rehabilitation measures should extend to everyday architecture, especially in derelict areas.
- Forgo two planned roads which would have de-stroyed the built fabric as well as the open space along the small river that forms the backbone of the urban development.

The recommendations have largely been accepted. Renovation work started in 2001. A total of 40 million RMB (US$ 5 million) is

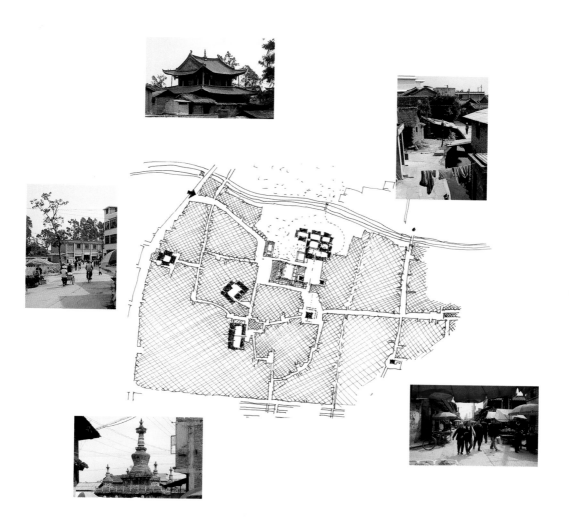

Guandu. Several temple sites and a central stupa form the main points of attraction in Guandu. The system of narrow lanes and squares will be retained. The proposal made by the group of experts emphasises the polarity between urban areas, lanes and spatially limited squares, opposite generous open green spaces. The backdrop of an intact ordinary architecture is of great importance for the overall experience of the historic village.

官渡。几座寺庙和古镇中心的金刚塔构成了官渡的主要景点。由窄小街巷和广场组成的格局将保留下来。专家组的建议方案突出了"市区、街巷、空间有限的广场"和"大型绿色开敞空间"之间的对比性。为了向人们展现一个完全古色古香的官渡镇，就必须重视对普通民居的保护，使其继续发挥日常功能。

安宁市

小城安宁市，座落在昆明以西35公里处景色秀丽的丘陵地带，海拔约1800米。它将成为缓解昆明主城压力的三座重要城市之一。目前，安宁市受重工业的污染很大，城市景观

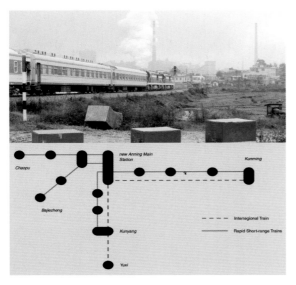

The site of the new railway station in Anning. A radially laid out Rapid Suburban Railway network centred on Kunming is planned. 安宁主客站将建在这里。已计划建设以昆明为中心、呈放射状向外延伸的快速市郊铁路网络。

则较为开阔。它的人口将达到50万（2020年预测数字），未来的经济发展将侧重于吸引高科技企业来此落户。政府有关部门打算依据可持续发展的原则修订安宁市的总体规划。

苏黎世专家组建议，安宁市今后应依靠快速市郊铁路体系进行开发建设。快速市郊列车将可大部分利用既有的铁道运行，而铁道同时还将服务于长途客运和工业货运。对既有的铁路网络将进行必要的改造和扩建，使昆明－玉溪间的列车能直接服务未来的安宁市商业中心。

available for this, mainly provided by the Province of Yunnan.

Anning County

The small town of Anning, 35 km west of Kunming, is set in an attractive landscape of hills, approximately 1800 m above sea level. It will be developed into one of three important satellite centres. This extensive urban landscape (presently polluted by heavy industry), where space for approximately 500,000 inhabitants needs to be made (by 2020), is to receive its economic stimulus from high-tech companies. The authorities intend to rework the master plan according to principles of sustainability.

The strategy proposed by the Zurich team suggests urban development along a Rapid Suburban Railway network, providing long-distance travel as well as industrial haulage, generally running on existing tracks. The railway network will be extended so that trains linking Kunming and Yuxi can directly serve the proposed business centre of Anning.

The concept developed in 2001 and 2002 proposes a new main station at Anning. The town centre of Anning, the new business districts east of the river, and the steel works will be linked in a triangle of new urban design axes. This new area is within the catchment area of the new motorway axes connecting Anning with Kunming, Yuxi and Dali. A prerequisite for success is the modernisation of the steel works. Optimising the land use requirements of the steel works would free up space for new uses.

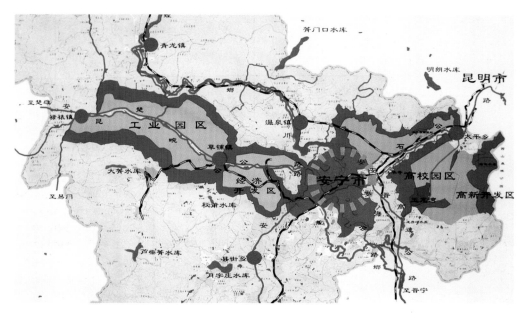

Anning County: the authorities of Kunming and Anning envisage a band of development from east to west which will draw its vitality from the establishment of new high-tech companies. The population will be increased from approximately 100,000 to 500,000. 安宁市。昆明市和安宁市有关部门确定了一条东西向的发展轴线，它将通过吸引高科技公司来此落户而获得发展动力。安宁市的人口将从现在的10万增长到50万。

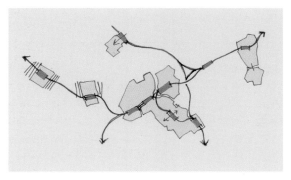

Anning: concept for concentrated development around railway stations. 安宁：集中开发火车站周围地带的城市发展方案。

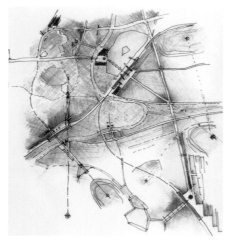

Anning: The central triangle of the historic centre, steel works and new development area forms the focal point of development, which is concentrated around the new railway station. It will respect the existing landscape (left). Site of the new central railway station (right). 安宁。安宁市目前的市中心、昆明钢铁公司生活区和安宁市新开发建设区构成一个三角形核心地带，它是安宁市未来发展的重心。开发建设工作应集中在未来的火车站周围，并充分尊重当地目前的景观（左图）。安宁主客站将建在这里（右图）。

根据2001年和2002年制订的方案，建议新建一座安宁主火车站。目前的安宁市中心、螳螂川东岸将新建的商业区以及昆明钢铁集团公司（简称昆钢）的生活区这三大部分，将由新的城市设计轴线连接起来，构成一个三角形的新市中心。它与附近的几条高速公路相距不远，这些高速公路把安宁市与昆明、玉溪及大理连接在一起。而实现这一发展的前提则是对昆钢进行现代化改造。昆钢优化了它的土地使用面积之后，将会有一批土地空闲下来，可以赋予它新的使用方式。

与安宁市的商业中心相呼应，应在安宁市的西部开辟居住区。这里将与相邻的人工湖"磷湖"构成一个新的中心。由于这一地区不受昆钢的直接污染，西部又面向丘陵地带，因而很适于发展休闲娱乐功能。

To complement the business centre of Anning, a new centre related to the residential areas in the west is to be created, forming a focal point with its existing artificial water body. Facing away from the direct influence of the steel works, many recreation and leisure facilities can be provided, incorporating the atmosphere of the hilly landscape opening to the west.

Along the axis running east to west, from Taiping to Caopu, 20 km in length, train stations are proposed where settlements already exist. Here, a concentric development pattern will be employed, offering space for the new high-tech companies as well as housing for people.

In the hilly, jagged landscape, there are some places where the river valleys open out, and some intermediary zones with moderate

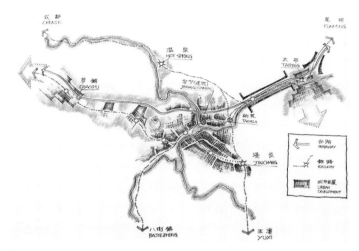

The new settlements will be placed according to the specific qualities of the Anning landscape. They will be separated by greenbelts.
将根据安宁景观的特殊风貌确定新居民点的位置。这些居民点将由绿色带相互隔开。

gradients which are suitable for settlements. Three important prerequisites for a high quality of life are: the uninterrupted presence of the hill landscape, the incorporation of rivers into the design of new neighbourhoods, and the structuring of the development axes by the use of open green spaces.

New structural plans have been developed, largely incorporating these proposals. The participation of a representative of the Kunming Iron and Steel Co. at the workshops indicated the interest of the company in playing a key role in the future development of Anning.

在安宁市长约20公里的东西向发展轴线上，将在太平和草铺之间已有居民点的地方修建几座火车站。开发建设工作将以火车站为核心进行，这些建设区既为高科技公司提供生产办公的空间，又为居民提供生活空间。

河谷附近地形起伏的丘陵地带，以及某些地势较为平缓的地区也适于进行开发建设。为了保证安宁市的高级生活质量，就必须让丘陵景观与城市直接相连、把河流纳入新市区的规划设计之中，并利用绿色开敞空间作为开发轴线的分隔元素。

现在，已制订出了新的布局规划，其内容大部分符合上述建议。昆明钢铁集团公司派代表出席了工作讨论会，表明了昆钢对该项目的兴趣，而昆钢将在安宁市的未来发展中起到关键作用。

结束语

我们的昆明朋友们没有多少考虑和等待的时间，他们必须立刻采取实际行动。由于发展速度太快，各种问题接踵而至，他们必须随时作出举足轻重的决策。我们很高兴地看到，在决策过程中越来越重视可持续发展的原则和提高城市空间质量的目标。最近新制订出的规划和项目便证明了这一点。

1 明代著名学者杨升庵曾赞昆明"天气常如二三月，花枝不断四时春"，故昆明又名春城。

2 昆明市政府于1995年致信给友好城市苏黎世市："多年来，昆明的社会经济取得了高速发展，城市建设突飞猛进。一方面，无论是旧城还是市郊，都拓宽或新修了许多道路，大量的楼房，尤其是高层大楼纷纷拔地而起；另一方面，一些具有昆明当地特色的传统建筑，或传统建筑集中的街道和街区却令人遗憾地消失了。有些虽然仍保留在那里，却面临着随时被拆毁的危险。这两方面的变革使昆明的城市景观每天都处于变化之中。这种变化非常突然、迅速，使市规划部门很难有效地控制城市景观。"

Conclusion

Our partners in Kunming know they have no remaining grace period. They need to act, and in the face of rapid growth and mounting problems, constantly need to make decisions of weighty consequence. It is fascinating to observe that the principle of sustainability, the aspiration to obtain a high quality urban space, is playing a role of increasing importance. Proof of this lies in the latest designs and projects.

1 'It is always as warm as February and March, flowers are ever blooming as if it were always in mid spring', Ming Dynasty poet Yang Sheng'an.

2 Excerpt from a 1995 letter from the municipal authorities of Kunming to the partners in Zurich: "For years Kunming's society and economy have been going forward fast and the city has been growing rapidly. On one hand, whether the old town or in the urban fringe, a lot of roads were widened or newly built. A huge number of buildings, especially high-rise buildings, sprang up on the ground projectingly. On the other hand, some traditional houses with local characteristics of Kunming or some streets or street zones, where traditional houses concentrated, unfortunately disappeared. Some are still kept there, but in immediate danger. Both changes made Kunming's urban landscape change with each passing day. The change came so sudden and fast that it was hard for the city planning authority to put the urban landscape under effective control."

JACQUES FEINER WITH
MI SHIWEN, DIEGO SALMERON, OLIVER LOUY, WILLY A. SCHMID
作者： 雅克•菲恩纳
参与撰稿人员： 米世文、迪哥•萨尔美隆、奥利弗•路易、威利•A•施密特

Regional Planning in the Kunming-Zurich Partnership

昆明与苏黎世友好城市合作项目中的区域规划子项目

Project Background

The goal of this project is to carry out and strengthen local and regional planning in Kunming as an integrated and comprehensive planning process and to support the planning authorities in Kunming in dealing with complex urban and environmental challenges. It was initiated mainly because the urban dynamics in the city of Kunming began increasingly to affect the surrounding rural hinterland, the Greater Kunming Area, which encompasses very sensitive natural areas, especially the Lake Dian Watershed Region. The risks of losing huge amounts of prime arable land and greatly increasing environmental pollution were obvious. Because rapid urban expansion started relatively late in Kunming, at the beginning of the 1990s we saw a unique chance to take advantage of the strong dynamics to direct urbanization towards a more sustainably developed path. As background information, the current development dynamics are very strong in China.

项目背景

本项目旨在实施并加强昆明的地方规划和区域规划工作，把这两种规划作为综合性的一体化规划程序来看待，并协助昆明规划部门解决城市与环境方面错综复杂的问题。本项目的提出，主要原因是昆明市的发展建设活动逐渐开始蚕食其周围郊区的农村地带，即大昆明区。而这一地区很多地方的自然环境却极为脆弱，滇池流域便是一例。大昆明区内大量的一级优质耕地面临着即将消失的危险，环境污染也日益严重。由于昆明的急速城市扩张从上个世纪九十年代初才开始，时间相对较晚，这对我们来说是一个不可多得的机遇，我们可以利用昆明强大的发展势头对它的城市化进程加以引导，使它走上可持续发展之路。总的说来，中国目前正经历着非常迅猛的发展，最重要的发展趋势有：
- 到2030年，中国人口将增长到17亿至20亿。
- 人口将主要从农村迁入城市。城市人

Population Growth (in millions) in PR China.
中国的人口增长（单位：百万）。

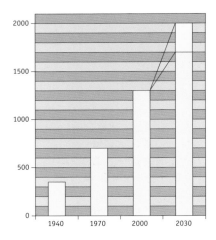

Motorisation forecast in PR China. 中国机动车发展预测。

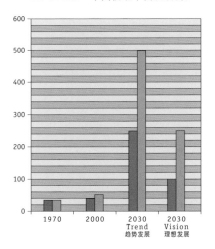

■ **cars per 1 000 inhabitants**
每千人小汽车拥有量

■ **cars in total (in millions)**
小汽车总量（单位：百万）

In summary, the most important trends are:
– Further increase of the total population to 1,7 – 2 billion people by 2030.
– Shift of the population majority from rural to urban. The proportion of the urban population (currently 30%) is expected to reach the rates of other semi-industrialized countries, that is, 70%. The urban population would thus increase by 0,7 – 1 billion. This will accelerate urbanization considerably.
– Dynamic economic growth (7 – 10% annually) and further strong change from rural to industrial and commercial workplaces.
– Rapid increase in motorcar use. If no transportation alternatives are established, there could be 250 – 500 million cars in use by 2030. These cars will require energy, roads, highways, parking space, and will be a major source of pollution as well. Furthermore, car-based transportation is the driving force in sub-urbanization and urban sprawl.

For city-regions like Kunming, the development dynamics accelerate at a greater rate than in China as a whole. Meanwhile, research clearly shows that current planning policies and approaches remain mostly those of a planned economy. The main characteristics are:
– Severe growth restrictions on the large cities and the active prevention of rural-urban migration.
– The active and strong promotion of car-based transportation, while neglecting mass transit and non-motorised transportation.
– Favouring small settlements and a highly decentralized industrial structure.

The greatest risk is that current development dynamics, planning policies and approaches will interact negatively and cause the loss of development potentials and synergies, while environmental pollution as well as traffic problems could get out of control. However, Kunming, like many other large and extra-large Chinese cities, has just started to develop rapidly. Thus, many risks caused by rapid urban development have not yet materialised or can still be reversed:

– Under current circumstances, the huge future population will lead to high urban land use. At the same time, the current land use pattern is still flexible and can be influenced by strategic planning and the preservation of fertile land.
– The change from rural to industrial and commercial workplaces is inevitable. The concentration of industrial production locations and the creation of large labour market regions has the potential to significantly improve economic and ecological conditions.
– Future urbanization rates will most likely lead to urban sprawl. However, transportation and settlement patterns can still be structured, thus reducing investment costs, saving commuting time and urban space, while reducing pollution caused by transportation.

To meet the challenge of future urbanization in Kunming, we took the following steps:
– Orientation of planning policies toward sustainability issues.
– Definition of a sustainability-oriented settlement and transportation pattern
– Reform of the planning framework.
– Implementation of comprehensive planning.
Below, we present this action strategy in brief.

Orientation of planning policies toward sustainability issues

An outline of planning policies, which have the potential to steer development on a

口的比例（目前为30%）将达到其它半工业化国家的水平，即70%。由此推算，城市人口将增长7亿至10亿。这将极大地加快城市化进程。
– 经济将获得高速增长（年增长率将为7%至10%），工商业工作岗位的比重将继续迅速上升。
– 机动车将飞速发展。如果不建立其它交通体系的话，2030年时的小汽车量有可能达到2.5亿至5亿辆之间。这些小汽车都需要能源、道路、高速公路、停车泊位，还将污染环境。另外，以小汽车为主的交通也是造成郊区化和城市恶性膨胀的最主要因素。

在象昆明这样的城市区域，其发展速度比全国平均发展速度更快。最近的研究结果清楚地表明，目前的规划政策和规划方法大部分仍是计划经济体制下的产物，它们的主要特征有：
– 严格限制大城市的增长，积极防止从农村向城市移民；
– 积极而大力地提倡以小汽车为主的交通，忽视大容量公共交通和非机动车交通；
– 提倡发展小城镇和极为分散的工业结构。

当前最大的危险就是：发展势头、规划政策和规划方法三者之间将会相互产生消极影响，导致发展潜力的损失和协同作用的削弱，同时环境污染和交通问题有可能失去控制。然而，昆明市象中国许多大城市和特大城市一样，刚刚进入飞速发展阶段，所以，城市快速发展带来的诸多危险尚未显露出来，或者还有矫正的机会：
– 根据目前的情况，未来的大量人口将会导致城镇占地急剧扩大。同时，目前的土地使用模式仍然很灵活，可以通过战略性规划来施加影响，拯救大片肥沃土地。
– 工业化和第三产业化是必然趋势。

115

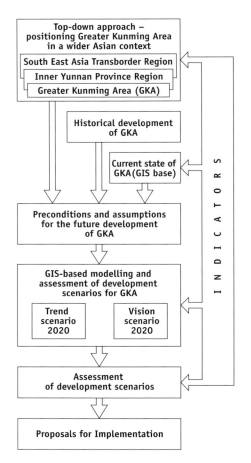

Research approach

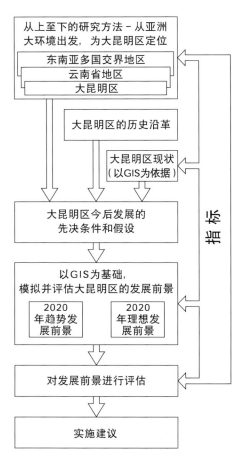

研究方法

more sustainable development path, is as follows:

– Promote large city-regions as future centres of population and economic activity.
– Actively prepare the large cities for their future role as agglomerations of regional size by:
    - Planning and co-ordinating settlement and transportation patterns.
    - Promoting a decentralized concentration of urban settlements inside the urban region, leaving green space in between.
    - Promoting mass transportation.
    - Promoting non-motorised transportation.
    - Promoting mixed use around city centres.
– Promote clustering of related industries and services at appropriate locations, and thereby promote innovation and control pollution.
– Minimise further spread of polluting low-tech industries in remote rural areas.
– Protect historic city centres and their original functions, by retaining the original population.
– Relieve the countryside of surplus population, especially in sensitive mountainous regions and other predominantly undisturbed natural areas.
– Protect prime quality arable land.

Definition of a sustainability-oriented settlement and transportation pattern

It is acknowledged that a well-conceived settlement and public transportation pattern reduces the need for car-based transportation and its associated negative impacts. It is, however, important to know how much these impacts can be reduced and what can be gained by implementing such a strategy, if significant investments in both money and labour must be made.

如能把工业企业集中在一起，并有选择地把某些地区建设为大型劳动力市场，将有可能大力改善经济和环境条件。

未来高速度的城市化进程将极可能导致城市恶性膨胀。然而，仍可对交通和城镇建设模式加以引导，以减少投资、节约上下班通勤时间和城市空间，并降低由交通造成的环境污染。

为了迎接昆明未来城市化发展的挑战，我们采取了以下步骤：

– 把可持续发展作为规划政策的目标；
– 制订以"可持续发展"为目标的城镇及交通模式；
– 建议修订规划框架；
– 实施综合性规划。

在下文中，我们将简略地介绍上述步骤。

把可持续发展作为规划政策的目标

能够将区域发展引向可持续发展之路的规划政策，主要包括下述内容：

– 推动大都市地区成为未来的人口和经济活动中心；
– 积极促使大城市作好准备，成为将来区域级的大都会：
    – 规划并协调城镇和交通模式；
    – 促进在大都市地区建设分散的城镇，但城镇内部将达到很高的建筑密度（多中心、高密度的建设方式），城镇之间将留出自然景观空间；
    – 大力发展大容量公共交通；
    – 鼓励非机动车交通；
    – 推动城镇中心周围土地的混合使用方式。
– 鼓励相关产业和服务业聚集在适宜地区成团成组地发展，这样既能推动技术和服务的创新，又可控制环境污染；
– 尽量限制污染环境的低技术企业继续在偏远的农村地区蔓延；
– 通过保持历史性市中心的原有人口，保护历史性市中心及其原有功能；

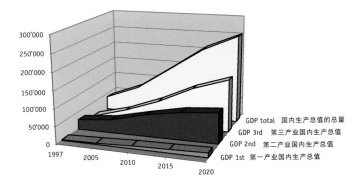

300'000
250'000
200'000
150'000
100'000
50'000
0

1997   2005   2010   2015   2020

GDP total   国内生产总值的总量
GDP 3rd   第三产业国内生产总值
GDP 2nd   第二产业国内生产总值
GDP 1st   第一产业国内生产总值

Gross Domestic Product in million RMB.
国内生产总值（单位：百万元人民币）。

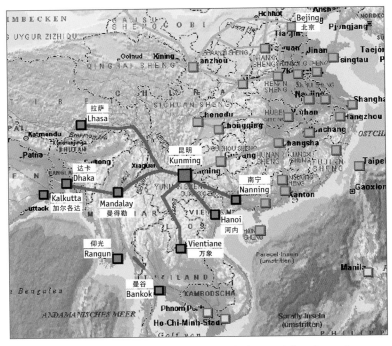

New transportation corridors. Orange for existing, red for planned.
新的交通走廊。橙色：已建成；红色：已规划。

Therefore, two alternative regional development scenarios for Kunming—a car-based 'trend development' and a 'vision scenario', backboned by a high-capacity short-range railway—have been simulated. The regional model was conceived by using a Geographic Information System (GIS) and the scenario technique. Relevant preconditions for these scenarios were:

– Increasing attractivity of Kunming. Since the early 1990s, a large series of cross-border transportation infrastructures have already been planned or are under construction. As they are realized, Kunming will be located at the centre of a far-reaching and well-connected transportation network. Because of this, Kunming has the potential to become the most important continental rail and road transport hub connecting China and Southeast Asia. With its international airport, Kunming's position will be enhanced even at the international level. This considerably increases the attractivity of Kunming for investment and immigrating workforce.
– Limited arable land. Of the Greater Kunming Area's total surface area of 9,654 km², only 1,071 km² or 11% is flat and fertile.
– Monocentric transportation network. The current road network focusses on Kunming City Proper and also provides very good accessibility to the eastern lakeside, towards Yuxi. This is the most attractive area for future urbanisation and has the largest share of flat and fertile areas, which are in danger of urbanisation.

Meanwhile, the main assumptions common to both the 'trend scenario' and the 'vision scenario' were:
– Same investments, gross regional product (GRP) and population growth. We project that the economy will grow by 5% on average and the population by 3.5% annually

– 减轻剩余劳力对乡村地带的压力，尤其是在环境脆弱的山区和其它基本未受破坏的自然景观地区；
– 保护一级优质耕地。

Kunming: starting point of the Road to Burma built during World War II.
昆明：二战期间修建的滇缅公路的起点。

制订以可持续发展为目标的城镇及交通模式
普遍认为，如能对城镇及公共交通模式进行良好设计，则能够减少人们对小汽车交通的需求以及随之而来的负面影响。然而，在投入大量人力物力实施这种策略之前，必须真正了解这种策略究竟能减少多少负面影响、带来多少积极效果。
为此，我们对大昆明区两种不同的发展前景进行了模拟。一种是按目前趋势继续发展下去的"趋势发展前景"，这种发展主要依靠小汽车解决交通问题；另一种则是依靠大容量快速市郊铁路的发展模式，即"理想发展前景"。进行模

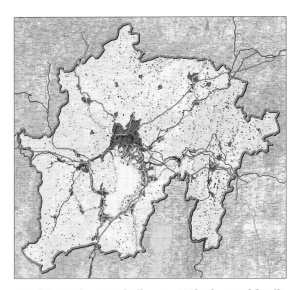

Trend Scenario 2020, built area 637km², use of fertile land 391km² = 37%. 2020年的趋势发展前景。建成区637平方公里，占用良田391平方公里 = 37％的良田。

拟时利用了以GIS（地理信息系统）为基础的区域模型，以及发展前景模拟技术。模拟时考虑到了下列前提条件：

- 昆明的吸引力持续增强。自上个世纪九十年代初以来，已规划了大量的跨国境交通设施，有些已在建设之中。一旦它们完全建设完毕，昆明将座落在规模宏大、四通八达的交通网络的中心。这样，昆明便有了发展成为中国与东南亚之间最重要的铁路和公路交通枢纽的潜力。利用昆明的国际机场，昆明在国际上的地位也将得到进一步加强。这将提高昆明对投资和人才的吸引力。
- 有限的耕地。大昆明区9654平方公里的总面积中，只有11%，即1071平方公里的面积为平坦而肥沃的土地。
- 交通网络只有一个单一中心。目前的道路网络仅以昆明主城区为核心。在滇池东岸通往玉溪的交通也极为便利，而滇池东岸正是对未来城市化发展最具吸引力的地区，同时它的平坦肥沃

until 2020. Thus the population of the Greater Kunming Area will rise from 3.2 to 6.9 million by the year 2020, the current low Gross Domestic Product per capita will triple, and the total Gross Domestic Product will increase six-fold.

- Same land use, population and GRP share per km² according to different building densities (rural, suburban, downtown).
- Same number of trips per day, same number of long distance commuters (10% of population), same costs of transportation infrastructure per km²; air polluters have identical characteristics.

The main scenario-specific assumptions were:

- Different development of the settlement and transport infrastructure: The 'trend' development will be based on road infrastructure and will further develop the existing monocentric settlement pattern. In the 'vision' scenario, a co-ordinated settlement and transportation pattern will be developed which relies on a railway network as the backbone. This pattern consists of a network of centres. It can be described as a decentralised concentration of settlements.
- In the monocentrically organised 'trend' development scenario, more people will live in suburban areas with medium density. In the multicentric 'vision' scenario, due to improved accessibilty, more people will live and work in central areas, which are built in high density.
- The modal split, the number of motorised vehicles, and land use for transportation infrastructures differs. This will result in different construction and maintenance costs, and air pollution levels caused by passenger

transportation will be affected as well.

Main results of the modelling process were:

The Trend Scenario

If urbanisation continues according to present trends, characterised by monocentric city expansion and based on motorised transport, new built-up areas will sprawl across rural areas in the vicinity of existing cities. Mostly flat areas which are easy to develop will be used for urban development. According to the modelling by means of the Geographic Information System, the extension of urban areas will increase to 637 km². Thirty-seven percent or 391 km² of the flat and fertile soils of the Greater Kunming Area will then be lost. Half the total population of the Greater Kunming Area will live in Kunming City Proper, and 70 per cent will crowd into the Dianchi catchment area.

The waste water of the 4.9 million inhabitants will continue to pollute Lake Dian. If the car ownership rate rises as expected to 180 per 1000 inhabitants, approximately 1.3 million cars will then be in use in the Greater Kunming Area, which will congest the urban network. By 2020, the transportation infrastructure will occupy a surface area of approximately 290km², which will tie up large amounts of investment capital and incur high maintenance costs. Air pollution caused by individual motorised transportation will increase dramatically. Nitrogen oxide emissions, for example, would be multiplied six times. In Kunming City Proper, traffic congestion is also expected to

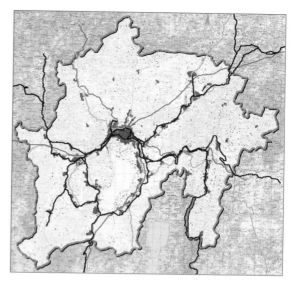

Vision Scenario 2020, built area 536km², use of fertile land 270km² = 25%. 2020年的理想发展前景。建成区536平方公里，占用良田270平方公里 = 25％的良田。

土地所占的比例也是大昆明区内最高的。这些珍贵的土地面临着被城市化进程所吞噬的危险。

模拟"趋势发展前景"和"理想发展前景"时，主要作出了以下对两种发展前景都有效的共同假设：

- 投资、地区生产总值和人口的增长率都相同。我们假设至2020年，每年的经济增长率平均为5%，人口增长率平均为3.5%。在这种情况下，大昆明区的人口将从现在的320万增长到2020年的690万。目前较低的人均国内生产总值到2020年将增至现在的三倍，而总的国内生产总值将达到现在的六倍。

- 每平方公里的建筑密度、人口和地区生产总值都相同。按不同的土地使用等级分类（农村、市郊、城市），每种地区的上述数值都假设相同。

- 每日出行量都相同。假设每天长距离上下班的通勤人员数量相同（占总人

Key figures for comparing development scenarios

Description	Trend Scenario	Vision Scenario	Difference in favour of Vision Scenario
Total population	6.9 million inhabitants	6.9 million inhabitants	---
Total settlement area	637 km²	536 km²	101 km²
Urbanization of fertile land	391 km² 37%	270 km² 26%	120 km² or 11% of the total fertile land of GKA
Land consumption for transport infrastructure	290 km²	245 km²	45 km² or 17% of trend land consumption for transportation infrastructure
Approximative cost of future transportation infrastructure	US$ 8 billion	US$ 5.2 billion	2.8 billion US$ or 25% of construction cost of new infrastructure
Population living in main centre of GKA (Kunming City Proper)	2.5 million inhabitants 36%	3.2 million inhabitants 47%	0.7 million inhabitants or 11% of total population
Population living in environmentally most stressed Dianchi catchment area	4.8 million inhabitants 70%	4.1 million inhabitants 59%	0.7 million inhabitants or 11% of total population
Water pollution (with identical investments in sewage treatment)	concentrated in Dianchi catchment	partly diverted to other, less sensitive water catchment areas	Reduction of water pollution in central parts of GKA due a more equal distribution to five different water catchment areas
Air pollution caused by households and industries	pollution is concentrated in KCP and the Dianchi valley	pollution is partly diverted to other, less stressed valleys	Diffusion of emissions in a wider area – reduction of emissions in central part of GKA resulting in an overall pollution level which is lower
Air pollution due to car-based passenger transportation: i.e. NOx-emissions for GKA	Depends mainly on technical measures		With identical technical measures emissions could be reduced up to 30%
Air pollution due to car-based passenger transportation: i.e. NOx-emissions for Kunming City Proper	Depends mainly on technical measures		With identical technical measures emissions could be reduced up to 50%

关于发展前景的关键数据

名称	趋势发展前景	理想发展前景	理想发展前景的优势
总人口	690 万居民	690 万居民	---
建成区总面积	637 平方公里	536 平方公里	101 平方公里
城市化建设占用的良田面积	391 平方公里，即 37%	270 平方公里，即 26%	节省120 平方公里的良田，占大昆明区内良田总面积的 11%
交通设施的占地面积	290 平方公里	245 平方公里	交通设施占地比 "趋势发展前景"节省 45 平方公里，或说 17%
未来交通设施成本预计	80 亿美元	52 亿美元	节省28亿美元或说25%的新设施建设成本
大昆明区主中心（即昆明主城区）人口	250 万居民，即36%	320 万居民，即47%	70万居民，或说总人口的11%
在环境最脆弱的滇池流域的人口	480 万居民，即70%	410 万居民，即59%	70万居民，或说总人口的11%
水污染（在污水处理设施投资额相同的情况下）	集中在滇池流域	部分转移到承受能力较高的其它流域	通过将水污染更平均地分配到五个不同的流域，减少大昆明区中心地带的水污染。
由生活和工业生产造成的空气污染	污染集中在主城区和滇池谷地	空气污染部分转移到承受能力较高的其它谷地	废气排放的地区扩大 – 大昆明区中心地带的排放量减少，从而降低整体污染水平
由小汽车客运交通造成的空气污染：大昆明区的氮氧化合物排放量	主要视技术措施而定		在技术措施相同的情况下：排放量最多可减少30%
由小汽车客运交通造成的空气污染：昆明主城区的氮氧化合物排放量	主要视技术措施而定		在技术措施相同的情况下：排放量最多可减少50%

increase, especially in downtown areas and on the ring roads. The city will lose some of its attractiveness for foreign investment and as a desirable living place for a highly-qualified work force.

The Vision Scenario

The vision scenario provided evidence that with co-ordinated transportation and settlement patterns, the development of the Greater Kunming Area could proceed in a more sustainable way. This is thanks to the clear advantages of the rail transport system: The passenger capacity of railways is up to 30 times as high as that of motorised individual traffic and provides an opportunity to sustain higher urban densities in areas serviced by railways. Furthermore, rail transport has clearly defined stations, which form nuclei and development cores. By doing this, the settlement pattern will form an efficient urban network with a clear structure.

Priority locations for urban development are train stations, which are situated in close proximity to existing marketplaces of regional importance. When fully developed, this pattern will consist of regularly distributed settlements with pedestrian-friendly centres. This pattern leaves open green space as a buffer between settlements, allowing inhabitants to benefit from nearby recreational and green areas. As a general rule, the new settlements will be situated at the foot of the hilly areas bordering the fertile flatlands.

Scenario Assessment

The most important advantages of the 'vision' scenario over the 'trend' scenario were:
- In comparison with the 'trend' development, 120 km² or about 11% of the most fertile soils could be saved.

口的10％），每平方公里的交通设施成本相同，空气污染的性质也相同。

针对两种不同的发展前景，作出了下列不同的假设：
- 不同的市镇发展模式和交通设施：
  "趋势发展前景"将主要依靠公路交通，并将继续按照现在的单一中心布局模式发展下去；"理想发展前景"则将采用经过协调的城镇布局模式和交通模式：它主要依靠铁路网络解决交通问题，并建设多座城镇，形成城镇网络，城镇内部建设密度很高。这种城镇布局模式可被称作"多中心、高密度"的模式。
- 由于"趋势发展前景"采用单一中心布局模式，相比之下，将会有更多的人生活在建设密度中等的市郊地带。而"理想发展前景"采用多中心布局模式，这些中心（即城镇）的交通更加便利，因此会有更多的人在这些建设密度极高的中心居住并工作。
- 在两种发展前景中，各种交通方式所占的比例、机动车的数量和交通设施占地面积都将不同。这将导致基础设施建设成本和维修保养成本都不同，并且由交通造成的空气污染水平也将不同。

趋势发展前景

如果城市建设活动按照现在的趋势继续进行下去，即继续扩大单一中心城市、以机动车交通为主，那么新的开发建设区将吞噬现有城市附近的农村地带。平坦的地带容易开发，因此最易被用来进行城市建设。根据地理信息系统的模拟计算，城市建成区将扩大到637平方公里。大昆明区平坦而肥沃的土地中，将有37％或说391平方公里的土地消失掉。大昆明区总人口的一半将居住在昆明主城区，而总人口的70％都将挤在滇池流域。490万居民的污水将继续污染着滇池。如果每千名居民的小汽车拥有量上升到预计的180辆，那么大昆明区的小汽车将达到近130万辆，它们将造成城市道路网的堵塞。到2020年，交通设施的占地面积将达290平方公里，这就意味着必须付出巨额的建设投资和高昂的维修保养费用。私人机动车交通造成的空气污染将大幅度上升。例如氮氧化合物的排放量就将增至现在的六倍。昆明主城区的交通堵塞现象预计也会加重，尤其是在市中心区和环路上。昆明市对外资的吸引力将会下降，高素质人才也将不再把昆明市视为理想的居住地点。

理想发展前景

理想发展前景证明，如能对交通模式和城镇布局模式加以协调，则大昆明区的发展将更具可持续性。这要归功于铁路交通体系显而易见的优势：铁路的客运量比私人机动车交通高出30倍；享受铁路服务的地区，可以达到更高的建设密度；另外，铁路有明确的火车站，这些火车站可以成为开发建设活动的核心。这样，城镇可以组成一个拥有明确布局的高效城市网络。

优先进行开发建设的地点，是那些位于大昆明区内现有重要集市附近的火车站。等完全开发建设完毕以后，各城镇将有规律地分布在各处，城镇中心都将设计得非常适宜步行者。在这种城镇布局模式中，各城镇之间都以绿色开敞空间隔开，使居民能就近去这些绿色空间休闲。作为一个普遍的布局原则，新城镇将座落在山脚下、平坦良田界外的地带。

对发展前景的评估

与"趋势发展前景"相比，"理想发展前景"的优势很多，其中最重要的有：

– The population of Kunming city proper will stabilise at 2.5 million or 36% of the population, while in the 'trend' scenario, the main city would grow to 3.2 million inhabitants.

– Much of the population pressure will be diverted from the environmentally sensitive Dianchi water catchment area to other areas (11% of the total population).

– The 'vision' scenario's surface area for transport infrastructure will amount to 245 km². Thus, 25% less road infrastructure will have to be built, which offers a saving of approximately US$2.8 billion in investment costs over the 'trend' scenario!

– Regarding air pollution caused by car transportation, absolute figures mainly depend on the technical measures and the legal regulations, which will be implemented. However, with the same preconditions, nitrogen oxide emissions from individual motorised transportation in the vision scenario would be 30% lower in the Greater Kunming Area as a whole, while in Kunming city proper the emissions would be reduced by half!

Reform of the Planning Framework

Research showed clearly that in order to implement a sustainability-oriented settlement and transportation pattern, the current planning framework and territorial setup would have to be modernised. Mr. Mi Shiwen conducted a large in-depth study to analyze the current planning system and worked out proposals for its reform. The key issues in this modernisation are:

– Reorganisation of the administrative setup. We suggest that the overlapping administrative hierarchies among the prefectural, the county and the local level be eliminated, especially the duplicate functions of prefecture and county in directly managing the main city or county seat, and that the whole territorial entity be abolished, as the overlapping responsibilities lead to conflicts among planning levels and hinder co-ordinated planning.

- Establishment of a corresponding territorial framework. The spatial entities and the division into planning spheres of prefecture, county, and community have to be set up in an unambiguous way. This is currently not the case. The administrative responsibilities have to be clearly defined as well, to ensure the proper functioning of the spatial planning system.
- Implementation of a local level in spatial planning. Currently the lowest planning level, the county, is too large to implement and manage local planning. Therefore we suggest that the local level, the communities (300km² in average) take over this duty.
- Implementation of co-ordinated and cross-sectional planning at the regional, sub-regional and local levels. Surface-covering and comprehensive planning has so far not been implemented in Kunming. We suggest, therefore, that on the prefecture level a regional guiding plan be implemented. In addition, a sub-regional guiding plan on the county-level, and a comprehensive local plan on the community level, have to be implemented over the entire surface of the respective territorial entity.
- Implementation of a monitoring and controlling approach for the regional and sub-regional levels.
- Institutionalising comprehensive planning in the People's Republic of China in the form of a presently lacking spatial planning law. There are actually many regulations and institutions which have something to do with spatial planning, but they are fragmented and therefore ineffective. The co-ordination of these regulations and administrations by

- 比"趋势发展前景"节约120平方公里或者说11％的最肥沃的土地。
- 昆明主城区的人口将保持在250万，亦即大昆明区总人口的36％。而在"趋势发展前景"中，主城区的人口将达到320万。
- 很大一部分人口压力将从环境脆弱的滇池流域转移到其它地区（总人口的11％将转移到其它地区）。
- "理想发展前景"中交通设施的占地面积将为245平方公里，这就意味着可以比"趋势发展前景"少建设25％的交通设施，相当于节约28亿美元的投资！
- 至于小汽车交通造成的空气污染，需视今后采用的技术措施和法律法规而定，目前无法计算出准确数字。然而，在同样的前提条件下，"理想发展前景"中整个大昆明区内私人机动车交通的氮氧化合物排放量将减少30％，在昆明主城区，它甚至将减少一半！

建议修订规划框架

研究结果非常清楚地表明，为了实现面向可持续发展的城镇布局模式和交通模式，应修订现在的规划机制和国土管理方式。米世文先生通过大量而深入的研究，分析了当前的规划体系，并提出了许多修订建议。其中最重要的课题有：
- 修订行政管理机制。我们建议取消目前地市、县和地方各级行政管理机构权责重叠的现象。尤其是地市级和县级部门目前直接管理所辖主城市或县城，我们建议取消这种双重角色。因为权责重叠的现象会造成各级规划部门之间的矛盾，并阻碍进行协调性规划。
- 设立相应的国土管理机制。地市、县、地方各级所负责的国土辖区和规划范围应划分得非常明确，目前还是这种情况。同时应明确界定各行政管理部

Greater Kunming Area basic land-use areas.
大昆明区土地使用功能的基本划分。

3 0 3 6km

Prime Agricultural Area 一级农业区	Other Protection Area 其它保护区	Open Area 开敞区
Other Agricultural Area 其它农业区	Mining Area 采矿区	Airport 机场
Urban Settlement Area 城市居民点	Forested Area 林区	Lake 湖泊
Rural Settlement Area 农村居民点		

Guiding plan for Jincheng. Example of GIS-based comprehensive planning.
晋城的指导性规划。这是利用地理信息系统GIS进行综合性规划的一例。

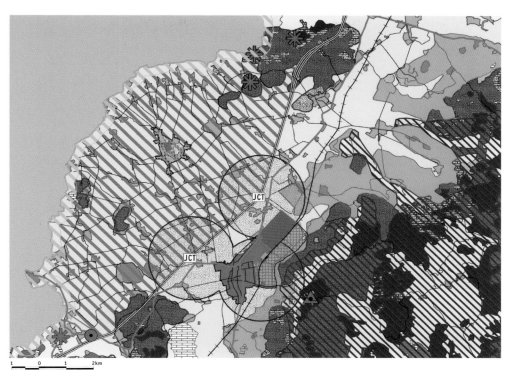

Existing Land-use Areas
目前的土地使用区

Planned Zones
规划的功能区

JCT Expressway Exit
高速公路出口

Scenic Spot
景点

Stone Statue
石雕

Temple
寺庙

Expressway
高速公路

High Grade Highway
高等级公路

Normal Road
普通道路

Planned Railway
规划的铁路

Lake
湖泊

Reservoir Intake Area
水库源流区

Forested Area
林区

Open Area
开敞区

Mining Area
采矿区

Other Agricultural Area
其它农业区

Prime Agricultural Area
一级农业区

Archeological Area
考古区

Rural Settlement Area
农村居民点

Urban Settlement Area
城市居民点

Transport Node Intake Area
交通节点源流区

Central Zone
中心区

Industrial Zone
工业区

Railway Station Zone
火车站区

Urban Settlement Zone
城市居民点区

Shoreline Protection Zone
湖岸保护区

Landscape Protection Zone
景观保护区

Reforestation Zone
植树造林区

Mining Zone
采矿区

门的权责。这样，才能保障空间规划体系正常运作。

- 实施乡镇一级的空间规划。目前最低的规划级别是县级，而县的面积太大，不宜实施并管理地方规划。因此，我们建议由地方，即乡镇一级的部门（平均面积为300平方公里）承担这一任务。

- 在区域、次区域和地方三个级别分别实施跨部门的协调性规划。迄今为止，昆明尚未实施覆盖全辖区土地的、综合性的规划。因而，我们建议在地市级实施区域指导性规划，在县级实施次区域指导性规划，在地方级实施综合性规划。在地方一级，应实施覆盖全辖区土地的规划。

- 在区域级和次区域级实施监测与控制手段。

- 建议中国制订《空间规划法》（中国目前尚不存在这种法律），使综合性规划工作制度化。目前有许多法律法规和规章制度都与空间规划有关，但它们过于分散，没有形成一个统一的法律，因此效用并不高。要想提高它们的效用，就必须制订一部空间规划法，把这些法规和制度都协调在一起。

对实施综合性规划的建议

为了以实例展示在大昆明区内如何实施面向可持续发展的居民点与景观规划（指导性规划），我们选择了"滇池流域"作为试点项目，它包括滇池周围的地区。我们使用的是经过校正的卫星数码地图，分辨率为5米。我们把这份地图与数字化的地形模型结合在一起作为基本数据，开发了以地理信息系统为基础的多层次规划体系。这个规划体系的三个层次为：区域（即大昆明区）、次区域（即县）和地方（即乡镇）。

要进行多层次的规划，首先必须建立详细的数据库。我们首先划定了核心

means of a new spatial planning law is therefore essential.

Proposals for implementation of comprehensive planning

To demonstrate how sustainability-oriented settlement and landscape planning (guided planning) can be implemented in the Greater Kunming Area, we selected as a pilot project area the Dianchi Catchment, that is, the region around Lake Dian. We used a corrected digital satellite map with a resolution of 5 metres, merged with a digital terrain model, as the basis for a multi-level planning system, which was conceived by means of a Geographic Information System. The different levels are: regional (the Greater Kunming Area), sub-regional (the counties), and local (the communities).

To manage multi-level planning, a detailed data structure had to be conceived. First, core and priority areas were sorted out. Then, based on the satellite map, the basic land use layers and the planning contexts were defined, according to the following structures:

- Settlement and landscape
- Transportation
- Supply and disposal
- Public infrastructure
- Lake protection.

Additionally, the Geographic Information System allowed us to set up an analytical section, to be used for monitoring and controlling.

On the basis of current land use and further planning information, the territory of the pilot region was zoned carefully. New urban development is carefully integrated into the scenery of the surrounding landscape and respects the carrying capacity of the local environment. Meanwhile, it is concentrated around the most accessible locations, serviced by high-capacity public transport located on second-quality land. This was made by using the following two approaches:

- The negative approach. All the areas that can be attributed exclusively to one certain zone and that should be spared from development are defined first (prime arable land, zones with human and natural dangers, cultural and natural heritage, forest and reforestation areas, etc.).
- The positive approach. All the areas and locations that are particularly well adapted to a certain kind of function (e.g. settlement zone on a regional level, or industrial zone on a local level) are attributed to their respective zones in a second step.

By overlapping the two planning approaches, by continuous consultation with the stakeholders and ongoing planning at the other levels, and by considering the background documents submitted by the different government agencies involved and the results of the basic research done by the different specialists and planning units, the local, subregional and regional guiding plans are formulated. The plans are composed of maps and documents and complement each other.
The whole planning process is designed and implemented as a bottom up – top down process. This means that the drafts of the different planning levels are co-ordinated with each other: The local level with the subregional level, the subregional with the regional and vice versa. The necessary timeframe for implementation, from start-up to finalisation, is estimated at three years.

地区和优先地区；之后，我们利用卫星地图确定了基本的土地使用功能；然后根据下列各点确定了规划内容：
- 居民点和景观区
- 交通
- 供应及废物处理
- 公共设施/建筑
- 滇池的保护

此外，我们还在这个地理信息系统中设立了一个分析部分，这个分析部分将用于监测及控制工作。
根据当前的土地使用情况和规划方面的其它信息，我们精心划定了试点地区内的土地使用功能区。新的城市建设区将巧妙地融入周围美丽的景观，并充分考虑到当地环境的承受能力。同时，城市发展活动将集中在大容量公共交通最便利的、属于次级土质的地带。在划定土地使用功能区时，我们使用了下面两种方法：
- "消极的"方法。首先，划定那些完全属于某种特定功能区的、被排除在开发建设活动之外的土地（如一级优质耕地、人为灾害或自然灾害潜在区、文化和自然遗产区、森林和人工造林绿化区等）；
- "积极的"方法。其次，将那些适用于某些特定功能的土地（如区域级的城镇建设区、地方级的工业区等等）划归到相应的土地使用功能区。

通过结合使用了上述两种方法，并不断与各利益群体进行了协调，还在其它层次上继续展开规划，同时研究了政府各有关部门提供的基础材料以及许多专家和规划部门的初步研究成果之后，终于制订出了地方、次区域和区域级的指导性规划。这些规划包括图纸和文字资料，两者互为补充。
整个规划过程都是以从下至上、然后从上至下的程序来设计并实施的。也就是说，在各个层次上制订的规划草

129

案都互相进行协调：地方规划与次区域规划进行协调、次区域规划与区域规划也进行协调，反方向亦然。从启动到最终定案的整个实施过程估计需要三年的时间。

结论

- 建议以覆盖全辖区土地的多层次规划方法，取代目前片面侧重城镇地区的地方性规划方法；
- 建议以跨部门的综合性规划，取代目前由于部门分割而造成的部门性规划方法；
- 建议行政级别及其权责与行政辖区相对应，消除各级间权责重叠的现象；
- 规划单位的规模应与其任务相对应：地方规划部门应设在乡镇一级，次区域规划部门应设在县一级，而区域规划部门应设在地市一级；
- 在每个级别上，规划工作都以可持续发展为目标。
  总之，上述关于综合性规划方法的一系列建议，都直接针对目前规划体制中的主要不足之处。

Conclusion

- The surface-covering multi-layered planning approach replaces the current selective and local approaches focussing only on urban areas;
- Cross-sectional comprehensive planning replaces the current sectional approaches shaped by a fragmented administrative framework;
- The administrative hierarchies and responsibilities are re-set to correspond with the territorial set-up; overlapping responsibilities are eliminated;
- The sizes of the planning units are made appropriate to their tasks: local planning is allocated on the community level, subregional planning on the county level, regional planning on the prefecture level;
- On each level, planning is oriented toward sustainability issues.

In conclusion, within this proposal for a comprehensive planning approach, many important shortcomings of the current planning system are directly addressed.

ULRICH ZIMMERMANN 乌尔里希·齐默尔曼

Co-operation in Supplying Potable Water
在供水方面的合作

The location of Kunming on a plateau, 2 000 m above sea level, automatically implies a lack of drinking water. Lake Dian, approximately 300 sq. km in size, had been thought of as an inexhaustible source, but is now threatened by the enormous population growth and by the waste water from increasing industrialisation that is seriously endangering its water quality. In 1986, the city of Kunming asked its partner city Zurich for help in drawing up a master plan for the supply of potable water and for assistance in finding the right method for treating water from Lake Dian to turn it into completely safe drinking water. This was the beginning of the technical co-operation between the two partner cities.

Around the world, the central design elements in a master plan for drinking water are

昆明市座落在海拔2000米的高原地带。一般来说，地势高的地方都存在缺水的问题。占地约300平方公里的滇池，曾被视作永不枯竭的水源。然而，

Kunming: Song Hua Ba drinking water reservoir.
昆明。松花坝水库。

随着人口的迅速增长和工业发展，大量污水排入滇池，严重污染了滇池的水质。1986年，昆明市请它的友好城市苏黎世市协助昆明市制订一份供水总体规划，并帮助昆明市选择一种将滇池水净化为安全饮用水的工艺。两座友好城市间的技术合作从此拉开了序幕。

131

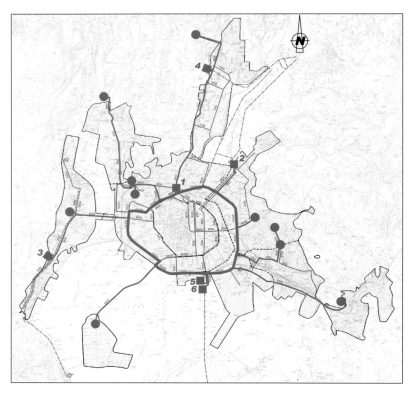

Master Plan for Water Supply for Kunming: general map.
昆明供水总体规划：概图。

世界各地供水总体规划的核心内容，都是设计大规模环形管网体系。每隔一定距离设一座水厂，把自来水注入环形管网，从环形管网分出的主干管道再把水输送到使用区。供水总体规划于1990年秋正式移交给昆明市政府。建设环形管网的思路得到了昆明市有关领导的一致赞同，因此，环形管网成为总体规划的第一期工程，很快便建设起来。

由于昆明市的发展十分迅猛，必须依照新的人口预测更新总体规划的内容。本来，按照总体规划原来的设计方案，完全可以依靠滇池解决昆明市

ring systems with huge internal diameters. These are, on the one hand, fed at suitable intervals by waterworks, and, on the other hand, have mains branching off, taking water to consumer zones. The master plan for drinking water was officially presented to the Municipal Government of Kunming in 1990. The concept of a ring system was accepted by those in charge; thus its construction could be implemented rapidly as a first stage of the master plan.

The enormous increase in population of the city later required adaptation of the master plan to bring it in line with the new population predictions. As anticipated in the original master plan, the great increase in demand for potable water could have been easily met by Lake Dian, since its volume is 1.5 billion cubic metres. The steadily worsening pollution of the lake with waste water caused a drastic reduction in its water quality, so that new sources of drinking water had to be searched for. Therefore, a joint project was planned for obtaining water from a reservoir located approximately 100 km from the city. Construction for this scheme for a long-distance water supply was started in the year 2001.

Also, the choice of methods for conditioning the raw water of decreasing quality from Lake Dian in drinking water-works developed into an active co-operation between the two kinds of water suppliers. It began in 1987, with the support of Kunming in setting up a central laboratory for quality control. Instruments and machinery were supplied and special care taken in the training of staff. The monitoring of all the main inflows into the long-distance water supply system for a host of chemical, physical and bacteriological parameters serves today as an example of comprehensive quality assurance applied to such a supply system.

日益增长的饮水需求，因为滇池的蓄水量高达15亿立方米。但是，因为污水越来越严重地污染着滇池，水质太差，不得不寻找新的水源。为此，双

Ozonized water after flotation and rapid filtration.
在气浮和快速过滤后经过臭氧处理的水。

Kunming Water Work No. 5 ozone reactors.
昆明第五水厂臭氧机组。

方共同制订了掌鸠河引水供水项目，从距昆明市约100公里的云龙水库向昆明市供水。2001年这一引水供水工程正式开工建设。

两市的供水部门还展开了非常积极的合作，寻求一种适宜的工艺以处理水质日益下降的滇池原水。这方面的合作始于1987年，当时苏黎世市协助昆明市建设了一座中心实验室监测水质。

Lake Dian: outlet gate at Haikou. Luxuriant growth of water hyacinths. 滇池在海口的出水口。水葫芦迅速蔓延。

苏黎世向昆明提供了仪器设备，并极为认真地培训了实验室的工作人员。掌鸠河引水供水项目中所有的重要水源都要进行一系列化学、物理和细菌分析，目前，这种方法可说是在引水项目中全面保障水质的典范。

为了试验哪种工艺最适用于处理滇池原水，双方共同进行了一系列调查研究和实验。考虑到原水的特殊要求，双方实验了一种效率更高的快滤池和其它手段。掌鸠河引水供水项目中新建的水厂就将采用这些技术。在成功进行了臭氧活性炭处理试验之后，昆明市通过国际招标建设大型臭氧水处理设施，瑞士的一家公司中标并完成了这项任务。

1994年，双方在昆明举办了首届自来水配水管网探管检漏国际研讨会。研讨会上强调了现代化管网管理的重要性，并探讨了维修现有管网的问题，因为这些管网经常会损失大量的自来水。

To test the most appropriate treatment or conditioning methods for water from Lake Dian, experiments and practical trials were conducted. To respond to the special requirements of each specific type of raw water contamination, efficient high-speed filters were tested and other measures were tried. These will be used in the new waterworks for the long-distance water supply. Based on successful experiments with ozone-activated carbon filters, the development of a large plant for ozonising drinking water was put out to international tender, and subsequently constructed by a Swiss company.

In 1994, the first workshop for finding leakage and the redevelopment of drinking water supply networks was held. It demonstrated the importance of modern net management, and was also concerned with the redevelopment of existing sections of a network, which were often suffering considerable loss of water.

HANS RUDOLF KRÄHENBÜHL　汉斯·鲁道夫·克莱恩比尔

Co-operation in the Field of Waste Water Drainage
在污水处理方面的合作

In the past in Kunming, waste water from households, treated only in septic tanks, was collected in local sewage systems, combined with rainwater from the streets, and discharged into the nearest river. Even today, the rivers passing through the city serve as collecting drains for sewage, which they carry to Lake Dian. At the same time that a masterplan was being

Kunming Sewage Treatment Plant No. 4.　昆明第四污水处理厂。

developed for the supply of potable water, a master plan was developed for waste water drainage. The first measure proposed was to treat the waste water from these rivers and drains in purification plants, to be built as quickly as possible. In a second phase, after the construction of the treatment plants, the waste water would be collected in newly built main sewers and flow to the plants.

The proposed treatment plants were constructed, one after the other, and came into operation during the 1990s. They were

以前，昆明的生活污水仅仅在化粪池中简单处理一下，通过污水支管收集起来，就与地面雨水一同排入附近的河流。流经市区的河流至今仍起着收集污水的作用，并把污水排入滇池。在制订供水总体规划的同时，也制订了城市排水总体规划。规划中建议昆明市首先尽快建设一批污水处理厂，净化河流沟渠中的污水。在第二阶段，即在污水处理厂完工之后，则应建设排污干管，把污水收集起来排入污水处理厂。

昆明城市总体规划 1993-2020

主城排水防洪规划图

DRAINAGE AND FLOOD PROTECTION PLAN OF THE CITY PROPER

N

1:25000

⊜ **Sewage Treatment Plant**
污水处理厂

KUNMING URBAN PLANNING AND DESIGN INSTITUTE

昆明市规划设计研究院

Master Plan for Waste Water Facilities for Kunming: general map.
昆明污水处理总体规划: 概图。

designed as full nitrificating systems with biological phosphorous elimination. After the treatment plants became operational, it soon emerged that it was virtually impossible to run them efficiently. The concentration of pollution in the waste water to be treated was extremely low, due to dilution with rain and river water. The construction of main collecting sewers, and with that, the separation of storm sewer drainage and sanitary sewer drainage, needed to be implemented as quickly as possible.

In contrast to running drinking water plants, the operation of treatment plants was completely new to the staff. In addition, the necessary laboratories to conduct required analyses were lacking. Questions concerning the operation and maintenance of treatment plants needed to be discussed with their operators, and an efficient laboratory established with Chinese chemists. The purifying efficiency and drainage values of the six currently operational treatment plants only satisfy the values set by Chinese authorities. It should be anticipated that the purifying efficiency of the plants will be further increased with the completion of the main sewers. Unfortunately, this is not sufficient for the necessary decrease in eutrophic nutrients in Lake Dian, so further improvements must be sought.

城市排水总体规划中提议建设的污水厂在上个世纪九十年代逐步建设完成并投入使用。这些污水厂的设计工艺都采用生物除磷和脱氮系统。然而，污水厂投产之后不久就发现，实际上不可能达到较高的运行效果。原因是污水与雨水和河水混在一起，造成进水浓度太低。因此，应尽快建设排污干管，把雨水和污水分开，提高进水浓度。

与自来水厂不同的是，污水厂的负责人员起初并不了解污水厂如何运行，同时也缺少实验室进行必要的分析化验工作。所以，苏黎世的专家与污水厂的负责人员共同探讨了污水厂的运行和维修保养问题，并与中方的化学专家一道，建立起了一座高效的污水厂实验室。从目前已投入使用的六座污水厂来看，它们的污水处理能力和出水水质仅能满足中国有关部门制订的标准。可以想见，一旦排污干管投入使用，污水厂的污水处理效果将会有所提高。遗憾的是，即使如此也不能有效缓解滇池富营养化的状况，还必须寻求其它措施进一步治理滇池。

全长14.3KM

霖雨桥至北站
5.2KM

The transportation system　交通体系

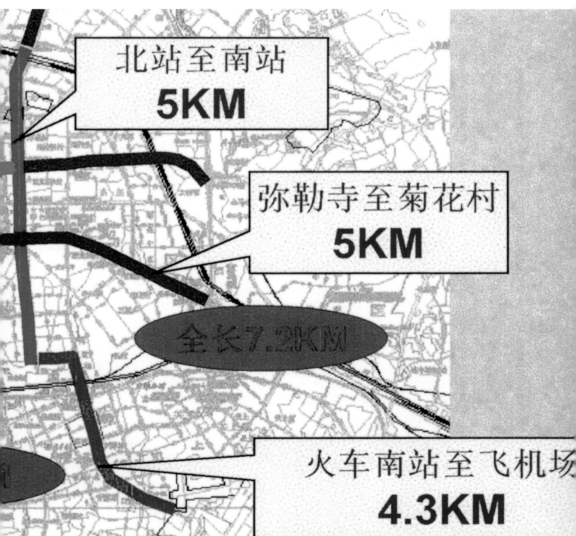

北站至南站
5KM

弥勒寺至菊花村
5KM

全长7.2KM

火车南站至飞机场
4.3KM

must move peop

nd goods, 必须保障人员和物资的流动，

not vehicles. 而非车辆的流动。

↑

小型
车道

CAR LINE

Giving priority 把交通优先权

to public transp

ation means 分配给公共交通，就意味着

moving the most people 运送最多的人

e least space. 而占用的是最少的空间。

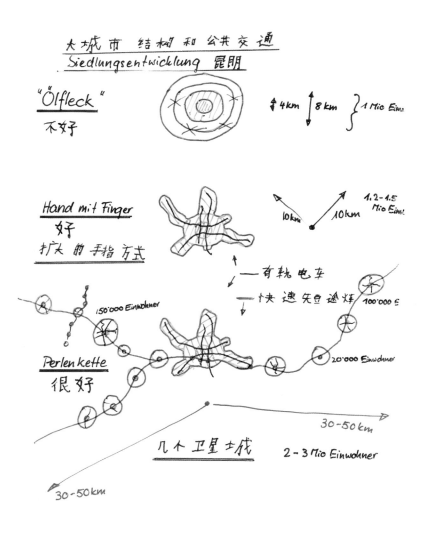

大 城 市 结构 和 公共 交 通
Siedlungsentwicklung 昆明

"Ölfleck"
不好

‡4km ‡8km } 1 Mio Einw.

Hand mit Finger
好
扩大 的 手指 方式

1.2-1.5 Mio Einw.

10km 10km

有轨电车
快速 轨道 运 输

100'000 E

150'000 Einwohner

Perlenkette
很好

20'000 Einwohner

几个卫星城

2 - 3 Mio Einwohner

30-50 km

30-50 km

The optimum model for the Greater Kunming Metropolitan Area is a Network City, with the city proper shaped like a hand, with the fingers as the radiating core, and a chain of satellite towns strung out along the existing railway lines. 大昆明都市地区的最佳模式将是 "昆明都市地区网络城市"，即构成以主城为核心、以沿既有铁路的一系列卫星城为辅的手掌状网络城市体系。

152

HU XING 胡星

Transportation Policies Custom-made for Kunming
适合昆明发展的交通政策

Kunming is presently in search of a way to maintain effective sustainable city development, respecting the economy, the environment, and society. To secure these strategic goals, an appropriate transportation policy is crucial. The 'vehicle-oriented' transportation policy will be gradually changed to a 'human-oriented' one. The basic ideas of the new transportation policy for Kunming are:

The transportation system must support the formation of a reasonable city pattern and structure.

The new transportation system must provide conditions under which the Greater Kunming Area can get rid of development sprawl, and support a finger-shaped development pattern along public transit arteries. Highly efficient, convenient, rapid rail transportation connections between the central city and satellite towns will be established.

The fundamental role of a transportation system is to move people and goods, not vehicles.

Giving the majority of transportation space and traffic priority to vehicles is absolutely wrong. It is a conceptual mistake that causes a traffic calamity in many cities. The

昆明市目前正在寻求和探索一条新路子，即如何实现经济、环境和社会三者兼顾的可持续城市发展。为确保实现这一战略性目标，必须制订与之相应的交通政策。交通政策将逐步从"车本位"转变为"人本位"。昆明的新型交通政策的基本思想是：

交通系统要支持城市形成
合理的布局和结构

新交通系统必须为遏制大昆明区"摊大饼"式的发展提供必要的条件，支持沿公交干线进行手指状发展。在中心城市和卫星城镇之间将建立高效、方便而迅捷的铁路交通联系。

交通系统的根本任务是实现
"人和物"的流动，而非车辆的流动

把最多的交通空间和交通优先权给予"车辆"是极端错误的，这是造成许多城市交通恶性循环的最普遍的观念误区。交通的本质在于"人和物"的流动，而不是车辆的流动。

在追求交通系统高效率的同时，
兼顾交通系统的多元性

在城市中，城市功能高度集中，而空间资源有限，道路不可能无限制地修下去。为实现城市功能、空间资源和交通活动之间的最佳平衡，根本的出路在于大力发展公共交通，实施公交优先，以最少的空间实现最大量人员的流动。

153

Kunming/Taipei: The capacity of a road, 42m wide, in persons per hour in both directions. Above, in Kunming, with 14m each for pedestrians, bicycles and cars: 24 000. Below, in Taipei, with 7m for pedestrians and 35m for cars: 14 000. 昆明／台北。一条42米宽的道路的双向小时运力。上图中，行人、自行车和小汽车各拥有14米宽的路面：总运力为24000人；下图中，行人拥有7米宽的路面，小汽车拥有35米宽的路面，总运力为14000人。

建设现代化的城市公共交通

世界各地大城市的经验表明，道路面积的增长无法跟上车辆和交通需求的增长。只有大力发展公共交通才是解决城市交通问题唯一有效的方法。昆明市和友好城市瑞士苏黎世市通过多年合作，把先进的交通理论和昆明实际结合起来，规划了由现代有轨电车、公共汽车和快速市郊列车组成的现代化城市公共交通蓝图。现在，昆明已经开始对公共汽车系统进行现代化改造，第一条现代化公交线路已取得令人振奋的成果。

purpose of transportation is to move people and goods, not vehicles.

While pursuing a high-efficiency system, attention should still be paid to the plurality of the system.

In a city, city functions are highly concentrated, spatial resources are limited, and roads cannot be constructed continuously. To realise the optimum balance between city functions, spatial resources, and transportation activities, the best fundamental approach is to greatly develop public transportation, and to consistently give priority to public transportation, so as to move the most people in the least space.

Constructing modern urban public transportation.

The experiences of large cities across the world prove that the growth of road areas can never keep up with the growth of vehicles and traffic demand, so that greatly developing public transportation is the only effective way to solve city transportation problems. In co-operation with our international friend city Zurich, Kunming has combined advanced transportation theory with the local reality. A modern urban public transportation blueprint has been mapped out, which will consist of modern trams, public buses, and suburban passenger railways. To date, Kunming has started on the modern improvement of the public bus system, and the success of the first line is encouraging.

Implementing traffic demand management in time and space.

The key to creating a highly efficient and pluralistic transportation system is the redistribution of transportation space and time at intersections. In Kunming, priority will be given to public transportation, pedestrians, and cyclists, while car traffic volume will be kept to a manageable level.

在时间和空间上实施交通需求管理
要实现高效率、多元化的交通系统，关键是要重新分配交通空间，调整路口的绿灯时间长度。在昆明，交通优先权将给予公共交通、行人和自行车。

Deal reasonably with car traffic in city centres.

The increase of automobiles in China is a fact. Traffic management policies can be formulated to deal with them in city centres, to keep their benefits without suffering from congestion.

ECONOMIC / ECOLOGIC DATA ON GLOBAL CITIES, 1990
1990年环球城市经济/生态资料

	Australian cities Perth,Adelaide,Melbourne, Brisbane,Melbourne, Sydney 澳大利亚城市 佩斯、阿德莱德、布里、斯班、悉尼	US cities Phenix,Denver, Washington, Boston, New York, Detroit, Houston,San Francisco, Chicago,Los Angeles, 美国城市 凤凰城、丹佛、华盛顿、波士顿、纽约、底特律、休斯顿、旧金山,芝加哥、洛杉矶	Toronto 多伦多	European cities Frankfurt,Amsterdam, Paris, Zurich,Brussels,Munich, Stockholm,Vienna, London Hamburg,Kopenhagen, 欧洲城市 法兰克福、阿姆斯特丹、巴黎 苏黎世、布鲁塞尔、慕尼黑 斯德哥尔摩、维也纳、伦敦 汉堡、哥本哈根	Wealthy Asian cities Singapore,Tokio, Hongkong 富有的亚洲城市 新加坡、东京、香港	Developing Asian cities Kuala Lumpur,Surabaya, Jakarta,Bangkok,Seoul, Beijing,Manila 发展中的亚洲城市 吉隆坡、苏拉巴亚、雅加达、曼谷、汉城、北京、马尼拉
Amount spent on roads per £1000 of GRP 每千美元.GRP(区域国民生产总值)花费在道路的数量	US$ 7.19	US$ 9.84	US$ 6.65	US$ 4.26	US$ 4.13	US$ 14.76
% transit cost recovery 公共交通费用回收百分比	40%	35%	61%	54%	119%	99%
Volatile HC's (kg/cap) 碳氢挥发物(千克/人)	23	22	22	12	2	14
Particulates (kg/cap) 固体颗粒(千克/人)	1.4	1.0	3.9	0.8	-	3.4
Transport deaths per 1'000 persons 每千人交通事故死亡数	12	14.6	6.5	8.8	6.6	15
% of Gross Regional Product spent on all modes of transport 区域国民生产总值(GRP)在全部交通方式上的百分比	13.2%	12.4%	7.4%	8.0%	4.7%	15%

Source: Prof. Peter Newman, Murdoch University, Perth, Ausralia

Cities that have an efficient public transportation system are the rich cities all around the world. Cities that invest exclusively in road construction are the poor cities. 在世界各地，拥有高效公共交通体系的城市也都是最富有的城市；而仅仅投资于道路建设的城市也都是贫穷的城市。

The transportation system must be economically feasible and environmentally friendly.

The transportation system must be economical. Both the construction costs and the operation costs must be affordable for the riders and for the city. The transportation system must also be environmentally friendly. When working to reduce the environmental impact by choosing between modes of travel, the allocation of space to different traffic means is most important.

小汽车的交通量将限制在城市的管理能力之内。

在城市中心区合理管理小汽车交通
在中国，小汽车的发展是必然趋势。交通管理政策应明确规定如何管理城市中心区的小汽车交通，以获得小汽车带来的便利，但避免产生交通堵塞。

交通系统必须经济实惠并有利于环境
交通系统应当是经济实惠的，其建设成本及运行成本都必须保持在乘客和城市都能够承受的水平。交通系统也应当是有利于环境的。与提高交通工具的环保性能相比，交通系统的组成结构对环保具有更为重要的意义。

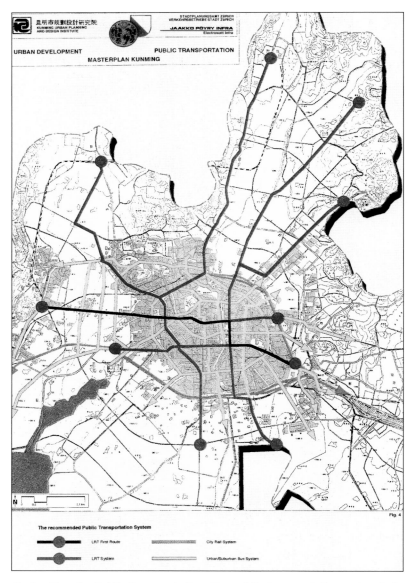

Master Plan for Public Transportation. The public transportation network for the city proper will be a combination of modern tram and modern bus lines, running on reserved lanes. The walking distance to the next stop should not exeed 500m. 公共交通总体规划。主城区的公交网络将由现代有轨电车和现代公共汽车线路组成，它们都将行驶在公交专用道上。从任何地点去公交站点的步行距离都不会超过500米。

MARKUS TRABER 马库斯·特拉伯

The Public Transportation Master Plan 公共交通总体规划

The first task in the co-operative urban development and transportation project was to create the *Master Plan for Public Transportation*, worked on jointly from 1993 until 1996.

Objectives

- Avoid unnecessary traffic by means of suitable housing development and land use planning
- Promote environmentally friendly means of transportation
- Develop an efficient and affordable public transport network
- Provide an adequate road network with efficient traffic management.

The stages of work on the Master Plan were as follows:

- Initially, a comprehensive household survey, traffic counts and studies of the traffic nodes were carried out. A rough estimate of the expected traffic growth for the next 25 years was made in consultation with the Chinese experts. The main objective was to analyse the present uses and resulting transport situation.
- Second, based on this survey information, possible transportation systems and networks for public transport were roughly sketched out.

作为双方在城市发展及交通领域的第一个合作项目，从1993年至1996年，双方共同制订了《公共交通总体规划》。

目标

- 通过制订合理的开发建设规划和土地使用规划，避免产生不必要的交通；
- 支持有利于环境的交通方式；
- 建设高效、经济上可以承受的公共交通系统；
- 建设必要的道路网络，实现高效交通管理。

总体规划的研究工作分为以下几个步骤：

- 首先，对许多市民家庭的出行情况进行了调查，并开展了对交通节点的交通量调查和研究。在中方专家的支持下，瑞方专家预测了今后25年的交通发展情况。这项工作旨在分析当时各种交通工具的使用情况及其对交通状况的影响。
- 其次，根据上述调查数据，初步设计了不同的公共交通体系和网络，以供深入研究。
- 第三，详细制订了主要交通工具的第一阶段实施方案（预可行性研究报告）。另外还制订了辅助性措施，如中心区非公共机动车交通方案、停车泊位的

LRT　轻轨系统

Bus　公交车道

Bicycle　自行车

Car　小汽车

Traffic flow in the city centre. Forecast for 2020.　市中心的交通流量，2020年预测。

– Third, a detailed development of the first implementation phase of the main transportation means, the suggested modern tram followed (pre-feasibility study). Further, secondary measures were formulated, such as concepts for private motorcar traffic in the inner city, maintenance of public open space, and transport management.
– At the same time, short-term improvements of the existing public transport system, run entirely with buses, was developed. Implementing such measures allowed the local authorities to gain their own range of experience.
– And finally, raising the awareness of leaders and experts was a very important task.

Some figures for the current and future transport situation

– In 1994, approximately 1.3 million inhabitants lived in the city of Kunming; by the year 2020 this figure will grow to 2.5 million. This increase will be mainly caused by a strong migratory movement from rural areas to the city.
– The built-up area will grow from 110 sq. km (1994) to approximately 225 sq. km (2020).
– At present, 1.3 million people make approximately 3 million trips daily; in the year 2020 there will be approximately 5.6 million trips made daily by 2.5 million inhabitants.
– The modal split will probably develop as follows:
  - Cyclists from 54% to 33% (at a constant amount of vehicles concerned)
  - Pedestrians from 33% to 24%
  - Buses from 7% to 30%
  - Cars/Motorcycles from 6% to 13%
– The number of motor vehicles increases by 20% each year.

经营管理、交通管理等。
– 同时，对传统的公共汽车系统进行了近期改造。昆明市有关部门通过实施这些改造措施而积累了有益的经验。
– 此外，帮助有关领导和专家树立相关意识，也是一项极为重要的工作。

关于当前和未来交通情况的几组数据

– 1994年昆明市人口约为130万；2020年的人口将达到250万。人口增长的主要原因是农村地区的人员大量涌入市内居住。
– 建成区面积将从1994年的110平方公里扩大到2020年的225平方公里。
– 现在，130万市民每天共出行约300万人次；到2020年时，250万市民每天总共将出行约560万人次。
– 交通方式的划分将发生以下变化：
  自行车 从 54 % 降至 33 %
  （假定自行车数量不变）
  步行 从 33 % 降至 24 %
  公共汽车 从 7 % 升至 30 %
  小汽车和摩托车 从 6 % 升至 13 %
– 机动车数量每年将增长20%左右。

提出的建议及其初步实施情况

公共交通总体规划不能只考虑到公共交通的问题，它对整个地区的交通规划都有着深远的影响。由于昆明气候温和、地势平坦，因此，步行和自行车这两种交通方式在未来也能够继续承担很大一部分交通任务。
分析结果表明，大力扩建城市道路网络、建设大量停车泊位以吸引机动车交通的做法，并不能解决交通问题。
未来的公交体系应是由不同的交通工具组成的、互为补充的网络。为了保证主要公交工具在未来较长一段时期内保持必要的大运载量，应建设轨道交通系统作为未来主要公交工具。在选择采用哪种轨道交通工具时，应考虑到以下

Recommendations and first steps of implementation

The policies of the *Master Plan for Public Transportation* should not be restricted to the field of public transportation. The plan has far-reaching consequences for transportation planning in the entire area. Thanks to its clement weather and flat topography, Kunming has a good chance of managing a large part of its traffic with pedestrians or bicycles, now and in the future.

An analysis has shown that a further large-scale extension of the urban road network with many available car parking spaces and the ensuing increase in attractiveness of motorised traffic is no solution to the transport problems.

The future public transport system must be composed of a network of several different modes of transportation complementing one another. To secure, on a long-term basis, the required capacity of the major means of transportation, rail-based schemes must be developed. The determining criteria are economic feasibility, phased implementation, and compatibility with the environment and urban scenery.

Working together with the Chinese experts, we reached the conclusion that for Kunming a modern tram would offer the best solution. This would provide access to the densely built-up urban area by building a net-like system of tracks, and routes following the finger-like axes of development to the periphery. The modern tram runs on reserved lanes along the roads; having short distances between stops permits maximum accessibility. It should be complemented by a finely meshed bus network, also run on reserved lanes, to reduce the walking distance to the next stop to less than 500 metres within the city area. Better access to

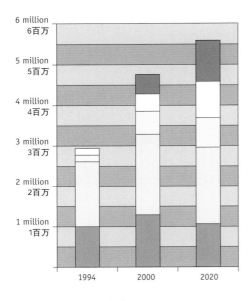

Traffic predictions and estimated flow of traffic, 2020.
2020年交通预测及交通流量预估

LRT   轻轨
Bus   公共汽车
Car   小汽车
Bicycle   自行车
Foot   步行

the Greater Kunming Area is proposed by improving the existing railway line to be able to run a Rapid Suburban Railway. It will connect the city centre with existing satellite towns, new towns to be developed at a distance of up to 60km, and even the new airport.

In 1996, a joint Chinese-Swiss planning group was founded for the implementation of the recommendations. The entire public network of lines was redesigned, a pilot bus route was planned for demonstration purposes, and a technical study on the first modern tram line was conducted. This first line, approximately 11.75 km in length, will cross the city in an east-west direction. It was designed for a capacity of nearly 8,000 persons per hour in each direction, and an increase in efficiency to 12,000 persons per hour and direction is feasible. Preliminary estimates put the overall cost at around US$215 million. The *Master Plan* proposes a track length of approximately 60 km. The implementation is expected to cost a total (preliminary estimate) of around US$1 billion. The construction time will probably be 20 to 30 years.

几个方面：经济上的可行性、分阶段实施的可能性、环境承受能力以及对城市景观的影响。

经过与中方专家的合作，我们认为现代有轨电车最适合昆明的情况。在高楼林立的昆明市建成区内，应建设方格网状的现代有轨电车网络；在近郊地区，现代有轨电车线路应呈手指状地深入郊区开发建设地带。现代有轨电车应拥有公交专用道，站点间距离较短，以便于乘客步行到达。此外，还应建设密集的公共汽车网络作为对现代有轨电车的补充。公共汽车也应行驶在公交专用道上。这样，在整个市区内，步行去下一个公交站点的距离都不会超过500米。在大昆明区内，建议对现有的铁路线进行现代化改造，建设快速市郊列车网络，把昆明主城区及其方圆约60公里内的新老卫星城镇乃至昆明第二机场连接起来。

为了实施上述建议，双方于1996年成立了中瑞合作项目办公室。该办公室重新规划了整个公交线路网络，并示范性地设计了第一条现代公共汽车线路，还完成了现代有轨电车线路一号线的技术研究。这条横穿市区的东西向线路约有11.75公里长，单向设计运力近8000人/小时，也可提高到12000人/小时。这条线路的总投资初步估计为2.15亿美元左右。总体规划中建议的有轨电车线路总长度约为60公里，总建设成本（初步估计）在10亿美元左右。建成整个现代有轨电车网络估计需要20年至30年的时间。

Land in a city is valuable. It is primarily required for places of work, shops and housing. Only limited space is available for transportation. U.S. and some Asian cities tried to go the other way, with disastrous results for city development.

城市内的土地非常宝贵。它首先要被用作建设工作岗位、商店和住宅。只有很少的空间可以用于交通。美国和一些亚洲城市曾尝试另外一种做法，却为城市发展带来了严重的恶果。

ERNST JOOS　恩斯特•约斯

Raising Awareness
支持领导树立相关意识

In China, city and traffic policy is more commonly formulated by leaders than in Europe. There is no contradicting high-ranking politicians; without their consent nothing happens. To raise the awareness of the responsible decision-makers and experts was, from the outset, an important part of the co-operative urban development and transportation project. The success of the project depended on their understanding the aims and principles of town planning. The interdependence of the basic functions of life and traffic/communication, the principles of urban development and transport planning, and the significance of comprehensive planning, needed to be described as vividly as possible to this circle of people who had been cut off from international exchange experiences for decades. In parallel with the technical/scientific project, workshops, discussions and visits for politicians and experts were held and new solutions were tested. Raising awareness with these people did prove to be an extremely important part of the project. Thanks to the trust that had been established over many years between key people on both sides, Kunming and Zurich, these discussions could take place at the highest level and show visible results in a relatively short period of time.

In 1994 and 1995, two seminars for politicians and experts from the city of Kunming were held, with lectures on contemporary

与欧洲相比，中国的城市发展政策和交通政策更多地受决策者意愿的影响。高层领导作出的决定是不容反对的；没有高层领导的首肯，下属也不能擅自采取行动。因此，从双方合作开展"昆明城市发展与公共交通总体规划项目"之始，其中一项非常重要的工作就是协助决策者们树立相关的意识。只有当他们了解了城市规划的目标和原则之后，项目才会有可能取得成功。在过去几十年中，中国的高层决策者们一度无法接触到国际上的先进经验。因此，必须尽量以明白易懂的形式，向决策者们介绍城市各种基本功能与交通运输之间的关系、介绍城市发展和交通规划方面的基本原则、解释综合性规划的重要性。所以，在项目进行过程中，除了举办技术性的工作讨论会以外，还与中方领导和专家展开了讨论，并组织他们进行了有关考察。此外，双方还通过在昆明采取一些可以马上实施、迅速见效的措施，共同尝试了新的解决方案。事实证明，支持中方领导树立相关意识，确实是合作项目中一个极为重要的工作。由于双方领导在多年密切的友好城市交往中建立了相互信任的关系，使双方能够在最高决策层进行交流，并在较短的时间内取得了显著效果。

在1994年和1995年为昆明市领导和专家举办的两次讲座上，以演讲报告的形式向他们介绍了现代化的城市发展政策和交通政策方面的基本原则。

163

Comparable area requirements for transporting 240 people by tram, bus, or car. This picture clearly shows the space-efficiency of the modern trams and buses compared to motorcar traffic. The efficiency of bicycle traffic lies in between modern tram and bus levels. 用现代有轨电车、公共汽车和小汽车运送240人所需要的路面比较。从图上可以明显看出，与小汽车交通相比，现代有轨电车和公共汽车能够更有效地使用路面。自行车交通的效率介于现代有轨电车和公共汽车之间。

1996年、1999年和2001年，在昆明共举办了三届"中瑞城市可持续发展及公共交通规划研讨会"，广泛宣传了在昆明的这一"试点项目"。来自中国全国各地的代表参加了这三届研讨会。会上主要讨论了下列课题：
- 可持续发展的重要性；
- 综合性规划的重要性；
- 各种交通工具的效率，以及因此把交通优先权分配给公共交通、自行车交通和行人的必要性；
- 保护老城的重要性；
- 在大昆明区，应沿现有铁路线分散性地建设一批城镇，城镇内部则应进行高密度开发建设。

principles of urban development policy and transportation. In the years 1996, 1999 and 2001, as a 'pilot project', three Swiss–Chinese 'Symposia on Sustainable Urban Development and Public Transportation Planning' were held in Kunming. These symposia extended the audience to include the whole of China. The following topics were discussed:
- the meaning of sustainable development
- the meaning of a comprehensive approach to planning
- the performance of various means of transport and the ensuing demand for prioritizing public transport, bicycle and pedestrian routes
- the meaning of the conservation of the historic town, and
- the development of the 'Greater Kunming Area' in the sense of strict decentralization with densely built cities along the existing railway lines.

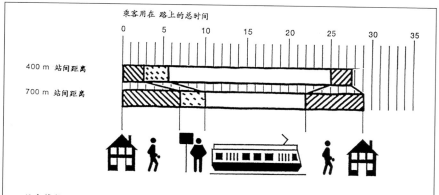

乘客用在 路上的总时间

| 0 | 5 | 10 | 15 | 20 | 25 | 30 | 35 |

400 m 站间距离

700 m 站间距离

一段中等长（4公里）的路程上出行总时间比较。有轨电车（或公共汽车）的不同的站间距离 站间距离短的有轨电车和公共汽车的行驶速度低于站间距离长的。然而站间距离短，乘客用在 路上的总时间还是更少，因为这样上下车的步行路程短，从而使乘客大量赢得时间（并且方 便）。

Long distances between stops increase overall travel time, because walking time — the least agreeable part of the trip — increases. 站点之间的距离过长，会延长总的出行时间。因为乘客的步行时间－－也是乘客在出行中最反感的一段－－将会延长。

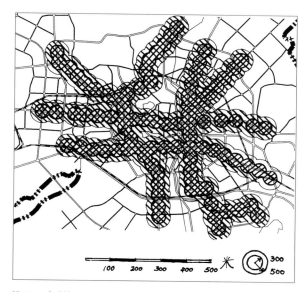

| 100 | 200 | 300 | 400 | 500 |
米

300
500

Network-like access to the inner city, with walking distances of 500 m. 通往市中心区的网络状交通联系，步行距离为500米。

另外，还组织中方的领导和专业人员，分批参观了欧洲的慕尼黑、维也纳、苏黎世、日内瓦和斯特拉斯堡等城市，使他们能够亲身考察现代化的公共汽车和有轨电车公司、先进的交通管理方式以及连为一体的大型步行区。

In addition, several field trips to European cities were organised for Chinese politicians and experts so that they could experience cities such as Munich, Vienna, Zurich, Geneva, Strasbourg, and others, with modern bus and tram companies, advanced traffic management, and large, continuous pedestrian areas.

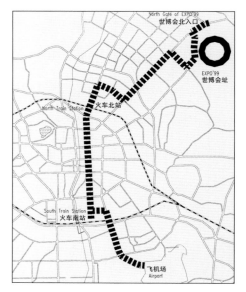 

The first dedicated bus route in China, in the central reserved lane, built at the expense of a car lane. The 'public-transport-first' strategy has not only improved Kunming's urban traffic conditions, but has also benefited the majority of the citizens and received praise from the public. 中国首条内侧式公共汽车专用道，它占用了原来的一条小汽车车道。民意调查表明，"公交优先"战略不仅明显改善了昆明市的城市交通状况，而且使广大的居民成为其受益者，得到了民众的广泛认同。

LIN WEI AND TANG CHONG 林卫、唐翀

Theory and Practice on Bus Lanes in Kunming 昆明公共汽车专用道的思考与实践

The First Step: 'high-quality-and-low-cost' bus operation

Kunming established an urban traffic development strategy designed to 'give priority to people's needs and public transit'. Taking into account its present economic situation, Kunming followed a strategy to modernise the bus system as a first step. Using advanced international theories and drawing on the experience of our Swiss friends, a high-capacity transit-only lane was planned, which would improve Kunming's urban traffic conditions immediately. In April 1999, Kunming successfully rolled out the first middle-of-the-street type bus lane in China. The second bus lane was built and put into use in June 2002, and a third and a fourth one are to be built in 2002–2003. Then Kunming will have established the efficiently operating core of a modern bus network. It is one of the basic characteristics of the bus lane design to look first to the passengers' needs, to safety and comfort. Improving environmental quality was another important goal of the project: reduction of noise levels, decreasing pollution from car exhaust, and improvement of the urban

第一步："高质量低成本"的公共汽车运营

昆明确立了"以人为本、公交优先"的城市交通发展策略。基于昆明现有的经济水平，昆明决定首先在近期内

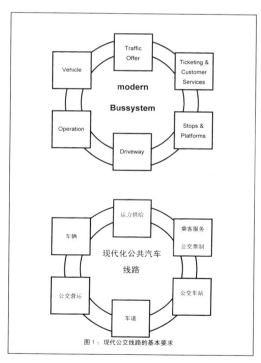

A modern bus system offers progressive solutions in six different areas. 现代化的公共汽车体系在六个不同方面都提供先进的解决方案。

对传统公共汽车系统实施现代化改造。利用国际上的先进理论和瑞士专家提供的经验，昆明规划了一条大容量的公共汽车专用道，以迅速实现昆明城市交通情况的改善。1999年4月，昆明建设开通了中国首条内侧式公共汽车专用道，并获得成功。2002年6月，又建成开通了第二条公交专用道。第三条和第四条将在2003年建设。这四条公交专用道将成为现代化公共汽车网络的高效运营核心。

公共汽车专用道的一个主要设计特点，就是它首先考虑到乘客的需求、乘客的安全和舒适性。促进环境质量改善也是项目追求的重要目标：即减少噪音和尾气污染总量，改善城市景观。昆明公共汽车专用道的建设和使用，对中国传统交通政策的诸多方面提出了挑战。它的成功运营，已经成为昆明城市交通发展方向彻底转轨的一个重要标志。它使社会和政府看到了解决交通和环境问题的曙光，并受到国内外专家和学术界的瞩目和广泛认同。现在，公共交通已为昆明更多阶层的人群所接受，增进了各种社会人群的亲近与交流。

昆明公共汽车专用道的设计特点

昆明公共汽车专用道布设于市中心最重要的一条南北向主干道（北京路）上，全长五公里。以前，由于交通负

Bus lane in a central reserved lane, built at the expense of a car lane.
内侧式公共汽车专用道，它占用的是原来的一条小汽车道。

landscape. The construction and use of Kunming's bus lane challenged traditional Chinese traffic policy in many ways. Its successful operation today is proof of fundamental changes in Kunming's urban traffic development orientation. It brings to society and government a solution to traffic and environmental problems, and has received notice and wide acknowledgement from domestic and foreign experts and in academic circles. Public transit today is accepted by people from more and more social circles in Kunming. It promotes familiarity and exchange among people from various social groups.

Design characteristics of Kunming's bus lane

The route of Kunming's bus lane goes along Beijing Road, the most important south-to-north artery through the city centre, with a length of five kilometres. Due to traffic jams, the road used to be a very inefficient transportation route. During rush hours, the average speed of motorcars was less then 12 kph, for buses less than 10 kph. The redistribution of Beijing Road's traffic space turned the road into a highly efficient passenger transportation axis, where buses now travel at a speed of more than 15 kph, independent of traffic jams. (At the same time, as a result of a new intersection design, safety and traffic flow for cyclists has been greatly improved.) The one-way transport capacity of a middle-of-the-street type bus lane is about 6,000 people per hour, equivalent to six ordinary vehicle lanes. Only bus lanes on the innermost lane provide these optimal running conditions. Using the outside lane, the buses would be seriously impeded by exiting and entering traffic and by parked vehicles.

The location of the bus stops has great impact on the comfort of bus riders. Taking into consideration the walking time of passengers before and after boarding the bus, we found that having a shorter distance between two stops would shorten the total travel time. Therefore,

Closely spaced stops at road junctions shorten overall travel time. 设在交叉口的大型站点会缩短总出行时间。

we chose an average distance of 541 metres between stops. Intersections make the most convenient rendezvous points for people and buses from all directions. The stops of different routes should be close to one another, to shorten walking distances for transferring.

Passenger safety and comfort requires platforms long enough and large enough for the rapid and convenient flow of passengers. The platforms along the bus lanes throughout Kunming are designed to be 65 metres long and 3.5 metres wide. These will also serve as the platforms for the light railway in future. They are arranged behind the intersection.

荷过大，这条路运输效率极其低下，交通高峰期的机动车平均时速只有不到12公里，公交运营时速甚至不到10公里。对北京路现有交通空间重新进行分配后，北京路成为一条高效率的客运通道，公交车辆不再受交通阻塞的干扰，运营时速达到15公里以上。内侧式公交专用道的单向运力约为每小时6000人次，相当于6条普通机动车道。只有将公交车道置于内侧机动车道，才能使公交运营达到最佳效果。如果在外侧机动车道上开辟公交专用道，沿线行驶的、出入及停靠的车辆等将干扰公交车辆。

公交车站的设置对乘车舒适度有很大影响。若把乘客乘车前后两端的步行时间计算在内，我们发现采用短站距能缩短总的出行时间。所以，我们选择了541米的平均站距。交叉口是最便于各个方向人流和车辆汇集的地点，因此是设置公交车站的最佳位置。不同公交线路的车站应设置在一起或相邻之处，以尽量缩短换乘步行距离。

为确保乘客的安全性和舒适性，就需要足够长、足够大的站台，使站台上乘客的流动既迅速又舒适。昆明公共汽车专用道上所有的站台都是65米

169

Traffic flow before and after the opening of the bus lane.

	Before opening the bus lane	After opening the bus lane		Increase and reduction
		After two months	After 2 years	
Car traffic flow**	1 840 per hour	1 326 per hour	1 611 per hour	-12.4%
Standard car traffic flow*	2 150 per hour	1 740 per hour	2 039 per hour	-5%
Passenger volume — Non publ. transp. vehicles**	4 233 people per hour	3 051 people per hour	3 921 people per hour	-7.4%
Passenger volume — Bus	9 936 people per hour	11 256 people per hour	12 000 people per hour	+21%
Passenger volume — Total	14 169 people per hour	14 307 people per hour	15 921 people per hour	+12.4%
Actual transport capacity of bus	11 040 people per hour	16 000 people per hour	16 000 people per hour	+45%
Occupancy Rate of buses (reduction means increase in comfort)	About 90%	About 70%	About 75%	-17%
Per capita delay at stops	68 seconds	46.2 seconds	47.9 seconds	-29.6%
Average speed of busses	9.6 km/h	15.2 km/h	15.0 km/h	+56.3%
Average boarding/ descending time	56 seconds	23 seconds	28 seconds	-50%

* all motorised vehicles running on car lanes; buses and trucks changed into standard car units
** cars and small vans

公交专用道通车前后交通量比较。

	公交专用道开通之前	公交专用道开通之后		增减幅
		两个月后	两年后	
小汽车交通量**	1 840 辆/小时	1 326 辆/小时	1 611 辆/小时	-12.4%
当量小汽车交通量*	2 150 辆/小时	1 740 辆/小时	2 039 辆/小时	-5%
客流量 — 非公共机动车**	4 233 人次/小时	3 051 人次/小时	3 921 人次/小时	-7.4%
客流量 — 公共车	9 936 人次/小时	11 256 人次/小时	12 000 人次/小时	+21%
客流量 — 合计	14 169 人次/小时	14 307 人次/小时	15 921 人次/小时	+12.4%
公交实际运力	11 040 人次/小时	16 000 人次/小时	16 000 人次/小时	+45%
公交满载率（满载率的下降意味着乘车舒适度的提高）	约 90%	约 70%	约 75%	-17%
人均延误	68 秒	46.2 秒	47.9 秒	-29.6%
公交车平均运营速度	9.6 公里/小时	15.2 公里/小时	15.0 公里/小时	+56.3%
站点平均乘降时间	56 秒	23 秒	28 秒	-50%

*包括在机动车道上行驶的所有机动车辆，巴士和卡车都以当量小汽车为单位进行了换算
**小汽车和小面包车。

Results of the implementation of Kunming's bus lane

The first bus lane in Kunming opened for traffic on April 20, 1999. An examination of the traffic flow before and after the opening demonstrates the results of this project.

Attitudes of citizens

In order to measure the attitudes of Kunming's citizens toward the bus lane, we carried out two mass observations. One was conducted after the project had been put into operation (1999), the other before the construction of the second bus lane (2001). In 1999, the total satisfaction rate of citizens toward the project was 79%. In 2001, total satisfaction was over 96% (active support: 56.3%; support: 39.9%; indifferent: 3.0%; objection: 0.8%). The mass observations showed that the 'public-transit-first' strategy in Kunming has not only improved Kunming's urban traffic conditions, but has also benefited the majority of the citizens and received praise from the public.

长、3.5米宽，它们设在交叉口出口方向。这些站台也是未来的现代有轨电车站台。

昆明公共汽车专用道的实施效果

昆明公交专用道已于1999年4月20日正式开通。我们对开通前后的交通流量进行了观测。调查数据显示了这个项目的效果。

居民态度

为了了解昆明城市居民对公共汽车专用道的态度，我们先后于项目投入使用后（1999年）和第二条公共汽车专用道准备建设前（2001年）进行了两次民意调查。1999年居民对项目的总满意率为79%，2001年居民的总满意率则高达96%以上（积极支持56.3%，支持39.9%，无所谓3%，反对0.8%）。由此可见，昆明的"公交优先"战略不仅明显改善了城市交通状况，而且使广大的居民成为其受益者，得到了民众的广泛认同。

Top: Typical street cross-section in the city centre: Baita Street.
Bottom: The newly built pedestrians-only zone in Jinbi Street.
市中心的典型道路剖面图：白塔路。新建成的金碧路步行区。

MARKUS TRABER   马库斯·特拉伯

Transportation Management
交通管理

Chinese cities have enormous population density. A proportionately large volume of traffic is dealt with on comparatively small road areas. Western countries have come to accept the new insight that a continuous expansion of the road network is not a suitable solution for the urban traffic problem. Sustainable transportation policy must aim at dealing with transport demands on existing roads.

Thus the efficient use of limited road space in urban areas is of particular importance. The highest aim regarding the economic power of a city is the transportation of people, not vehicles. This aim requires the use of space-efficient means of transportation and modern transportation management. Only with the use of environmentally friendly types of transportation, such as pedestrians, bicycles, and public transit, can toxic emissions be limited or reduced in city centres.

The road area of the city of Kunming has increased dramatically over the past ten years. Today, wide roads of four to six lanes of motorised traffic with bicycle lanes at the sides and pedestrian pavements dominate the appearance of the city centre. New roads will be 40 metres wide, or even more.

The city authorities have realised that the expansion of the road network is ultimately no solution to their transportation problems.

中国城市的人口密度极高，因而交通量也非常大，然而道路面积却相对较小。西方国家目前普遍接受了这样一个新观点，就是一味扩建道路网络并不能解决城市的交通问题，可持续交通政策必须旨在依靠现有的道路面积满足交通需求。

因此，尽量使城市中有限的道路面积发挥最大的效率，具有十分重要的意义。就城市的经济实力而言，交通的最高目标应是实现大量人员的流动，而并非大量车辆的流动。要实现这一目标，就必须使用道路面积利用率最高的交通工具，并采取先进的交通管理手段。只有支持有利于环境的交通方式，即步行、自行车和公共交通，才能在市中心地带限制或减少废气排放量。

然而，昆明市政府却发现，扩建道路网络并不能解决交通问题。因此，昆明市决定采取交通管理手段，更合理地利用现有的道路面积。

昆明市在东风路和北京路上开辟了公共汽车专用道，在其中某些路段上为此而减少了机动车道。另外几条交通干道上也将采取这种措施。公交车辆在交叉口也将可以优先通行。现在，公共汽车在某些地带就允许使用左转车道向前直行。昆明还将采用一种先进的管理系统：公共汽车驶近路口时，信号灯控制系统便可接收到该车辆即

A junction controlled by traffic lights before and after improvements. In the picture below, the new bus route in the central reserved lane has been implemented. 一个由交通信号灯控制的路口在实施改善措施前后的情况比较。在下图中，新修建的内侧式公共汽车专用道已建设完毕。

The existing roads are thus be utilised best through focussed transport management.

On Dongfeng and Beijing Streets, bus lanes were reserved, partly leading to the reduction of lanes for motorised traffic. These measures are planned for other main roads as well. Public transport vehicles should also be favoured at junctions. Today, buses are allowed in some places to continue straight ahead from the left-turn lane. A system is planned by which a bus can be registered by the traffic light control so as to trigger the green light at the appropriate time.

At the beginning of the work in Kunming, bicycles were regarded as a hindrance to the flow of traffic and it was intended to rigorously decrease their numbers. In 1995, the first junction control became operational, including a separate phase for left turning traffic, including bicycles, which represented a pioneering feat for the People's Republic of China. This markedly improved the flow of traffic at junctions and increased the safety for bicycles, which ceased to be a traffic nuisance.

The creation of pedestrian zones, to be further extended in future, has made the city centre much more attractive to pedestrians. With the planned improvements to pedestrian

将到达路口的信息，并适时将信号灯换成绿灯，让公共汽车优先通行。

项目开展的初期，昆明认为自行车是对交通的干扰，因此打算严格限制自行车的数量。后来，昆明于1995年对一个路口首次实施了新型的路口渠化设计，为左转的车辆（包括自行车在内）设置了专门的信号灯，这是中国国内第一次采取这种措施。路口进行渠化后，车辆通行能力有了显著改

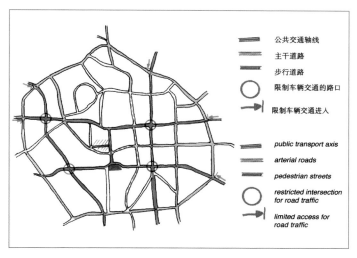

Today the urban structure of Kunming is defined by certain main road axes. The atmospheric quality on the important roads and squares should be improved. Therefore the inflow of traffic and the transit traffic must be limited.
目前，昆明的城市布局是由某些主要道路轴线确定的。应改善这些重要道路和广场的氛围。因此，必须限制这里的入境和过境交通。

观，自行车的安全性大大提高，自行车也不再干扰交通了。

开辟了步行区以后，市中心对行人的吸引力明显提高。昆明市将来还要开辟更多的步行区。另外，昆明还计划改善重要道路的行人过路条件（如建设安全岛、设置信号灯控制系统等），

从而把步行道路连成一个网络，以提高整个市中心地区行人的安全，保障行人的流动。

crossings on major roads (construction of central islands, installation of traffic light controls), a coherent network of pedestrian paths will re-emerge, safeguarding and securing pedestrian mobility in its entirety within the centre.

Numerous pedestrian traffic islands for safely crossing main roads help make the city more attractive to pedestrians. 在主要道路上修建大量的行人安全岛，保障行人的过路安全，可以提高城市对步行的吸引力。

Bicycle traffic moves a high number of people using relatively little space. 自行车交通可以利用很少的空间完成大量人员的流动。

GOU JINSUO   荀金锁

The Urban Rail Communication System
城市轨道交通体系

Rapid Suburb Railway is easy to implent

With the development of the Greater Kunming Area into a large metropolis, the question arises as to how we can best deal with the transportation requirements between the major city and its satellites. To escape the problems of using only expressways, with the attendant traffic jams and serious air pollution, we have decided to use the existing railway network for this task. We will reconstruct the present railway to meet the requirements of Rapid Suburban Railway by improving the existing tracks. This will offer considerable advantages:

– The present railway lines form a radiating network that links the city centre with its suburban areas. By upgrading the lines, the stops, and the affiliated signal facilities, and using state-of-the-art rolling stock, it will become possible for this network to undertake bulk transport volume in an efficient, safe and comfortable manner.
– The existing railway is a huge fixed asset, the result of years of construction

快速市郊列车便于实施

大昆明区将建成一个大都市圈。这个发展也带来了一个新的课题，就是如何解决主城与卫星城之间的交通联系。如果仅仅采用高速公路作为交通

The new Rapid Suburban Railway is mainly based on existing railway tracks. 新型的快速市郊铁路服务主要以既有铁路为依托。

骨干，将造成交通堵塞并严重污染环境。为避免这些问题，我们决定利用既有铁路网来承担这个任务。我们将对现有铁路进行必要的改造，增加快速市郊列车新业务。这个方案具有突出的优势：

– 现有铁路线在空间上的分布呈环状和放射状，正好将主城区和其它城镇串

连起来。经过对线路、车站和信号设施的升级改造后，配以先进的车辆设备，这一网络即能够承担高效、安全、舒适的大运量交通业务。

- 既有铁路经过多年的建设和维护，形成了数额巨大的固定资产，仅需进行

A modern suburban train in Kunming.
昆明的一列现代化市郊列车。

某些扩建即可。以昆明至嵩明的40公里铁路为例，若新建一条铁路，将需要近30亿人民币（合3.75亿美元）；而对既有铁路的改造工作则仅需要10亿人民币（合1.25亿美元）左右。

- 利用现有铁路经营快速市郊列车，而不是修建新的高速公路，可节省大量的土地，其中耕地和林地约占80％。这对于山地多、耕地后备资源紧缺的云南省来说，无疑具有巨大的生态效益和社会效益。

- 铁路有利于环境质量的提高。铁路节约能源，不排放废气，其产生的噪声可通过适当的措施加以限制。

- 铁路部门必须适应社会主义市场经济的要求。如能开拓城市、城际间的短途公交客运市场，铁路局将获得新的收入来源。根据昆明市总体规划，预测昆明与嵩明间单向客流2015年可达

and maintenance, and only needs completion. Taking the 40 km railway from Kunming to Songming as an example, a new railway would cost roughly 3 billion RMB (US$375 million), as compared to the improvement of the existing railway, which would cost only about 1 billion RMB (US$125 million).

- If we use the improved railway lines for Rapid Suburban Railway instead of building new expressways, we reduce the land occupancy by many square kilometres. This land contains about 80% arable land and forest. This implies great ecological and social benefits in a province like Yunnan, which lacks arable land due to its mountainous topography.

- The railway is environmentally friendly. It saves energy, it does not pollute, and its noise can be properly controlled.

- The railway has to comply with the socialist market economy. By developing a Rapid Suburban Railway to serve city regions, the railway bureau gains a new income source. Planning for Kunming for the year 2015 predicts a one-way passenger flow between Kunming and Songming of 17,000,000 people. This is a long-term and stable passenger source, a promising market prospect.

Preparations for implementation

As a first step, we will upgrade the Songming – Kunming line, add service to the new airport as well. For this, we have made already the following preparations:

- The Kunming South Railway Station will be expanded in the next two years. The possibility of opening a Rapid Suburban Railway has been taken into consideration. In addition to the increased capacity for long-distance trains, it will have a special platform with a special corridor for passengers entering and leaving the suburban trains.

– Double-track construction on the Kunming–Songming Line has already been arranged by the Ministry of Railways, to be built during the Tenth Five-Year Plan. The new layout will allow an operating velocity of 120 kph. With the additional track, there will be enough capacity for Rapid Suburban trains, and for additional stops in the centres of newly designed towns and at the new international airport. At train stations we have taken into account ways to make comfortable, convenient connections with feeder bus lines.

– In addition, for the narrow gauge railway section from Shizui in the west of Kunming to Chenggong in the east, via the northern part of Kunming, we have carried out some preliminary studies for passenger train operations, including the transformation investment, operating costs, and transport revenue generated.

1700万人次，而且具有长期、稳定的特点，市场前景十分看好。

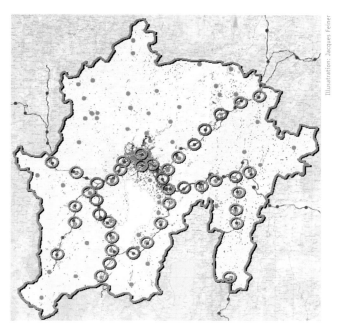

Railway stations and market areas for short-term needs in proximity. 短途客运火车站和集市概览。

实施准备

我们将率先开行昆明与嵩明（含新机场）之间的快速市郊列车。为此，我们已开展了下列准备工作：

位于昆明南部的昆明客站将在今后两年内进行扩建。扩建工程已将开行快速市郊列车的条件考虑在内。除了提高接发长途旅客列车的能力外，还将建设专用的快速市郊列车站台和客流通道。

在铁道部的"十五"计划中，安排了昆明至嵩明段复线的建设。建成后的最高运行速度为120公里/小时。复线建成后，可以满足开行快速市郊列车的条件，并将在新设计的城镇中心和新国际机场设立新火车站。我们也考虑到了车站与当地公共汽车线路之间舒适的换乘条件。

Elevated station in Singapore, with bus connections at street level.
新加坡的高架火车站，地面上有公共汽车站与之相连。

另外，针对窄轨铁路上西起石咀、经昆明北、东至呈贡的一段，我们已初步研究了开行客运列车的可能性，包括改造投资、运营成本和运输收入等方面。

展望

将既有铁路改造后兼容快速市郊列车，是一项巨大的挑战，不仅需要解决技术问题，还应组织政府和铁路部门展开合作。铁路和城市的发展互相依托、互相促进的作用十分明显。为使这个新型的发展蓝图变为现实，政府有关部门应引导经济区和居民区沿铁路轴线进行建设，并应在建设投资、运营补贴和政策支持上采取相应对策。

Outlook

It is a big challenge to improve the existing railway to make the Rapid Suburban Railway feasible. As well as solving technical problems, co-operation between governments and the railway has to be organised. It is clear that the development of the railway and urbanisation depend upon each other. To guarantee the success of the new development scheme, the relevant governmental departments will have to guide economic zones and residential quarters to be constructed along the axis of the railway line, and will have to produce policies supporting construction investment, operational allowances and policy backup.

ERNST JOOS   恩斯特·约斯

The Modern Tram in Dalian
现代有轨电车在大连

Our joint project with the city of Kunming received more than half its financing from the Swiss Confederation, represented by the Swiss Agency for Development and Co-operation (SDC). This organisation was eager to ensure the usefulness of this pilot project to other cities in China. Part of the project was thus to make available the results of the work in Kunming to other cities. Links to Beijing, Shanghai, Nanjing, Guangzhou, Changchun, Lanzhou, Shenyang and Dalian were formed. While the results of exchanges of ideas are generally hard to measure, this was not the case in Dalian, the third most important port city in the northeast of China.

We knew that Dalian was almost the only city still operating a tram network (Changchun also operates one tram line). With the intention of creating synergies for the tram project in Kunming, a small technical delegation from Switzerland visited Dalian in the autumn of 1997. This one visit led to others. The first delegation was reluctantly shown

在我们与昆明市的合作项目上，代表瑞士联邦政府的瑞士联邦发展与合作司承担了超过半数的瑞方项目费用。发展与合作司希望把合作项目作为一

Articulated low-floor tram developed and built in Dalian, China. 中国大连制造的低地板、铰链式现代有轨电车。

个试点项目来看待，将项目的成功经验推广到中国的其它城市。因此，项目中的一个重要工作就是向中国的其它城市介绍我们在昆明的工作成果。出于这个原因，我们与北京、上海、南京、广州、长春、兰州、沈阳和大连等城市建立了联系。一般来说，这种思想交流带来的直接效果很难测量。可是，在位于中国东北的中国第三大港口城市大连市，情况却不相同。

据我们当时了解，大连几乎是中国唯一一座还保留着有轨电车网络的

New construction for the modernised tram network in Dalian.
大连有轨电车网络现代化改造项目中的新建工程。

城市（长春市也有一条有轨电车线路）。为了发挥昆明市现代有轨电车项目的协同作用，瑞士方面派出了一个小型技术代表团于1997年秋季访问了大连市。其后，我们又多次派代表团出访大连。第一个代表团访问大连时，大连方面只是很不情愿地向我们介绍了保留下来的有轨电车网络，并认为它是一种过时的、应当拆除的东西。与此相反，大连向我们介绍了它的目标：一个现代化地铁项目。然而，我们成功地使大连方面对有轨电车（当然是经过现代化改造之后的现代有轨电车）建立了信心。大连派出了两批技术代表团访问苏黎世，甚至市长先生也对此产生了浓厚兴趣，并应邀到苏黎世访问。在访问即将结束时，大连市市长宣布：通过对苏黎世的访问，他坚信现代有轨电车是最适合大连市的交通工具。大连将全力以赴，对保留下来的有轨电车网络进行现代化改造和扩建。

事实证明市长先生是以非常严肃认真的态度讲这番话的，并以不同寻常的努力实现了这个愿望：当我们于2000年10月赴大连进行技术交流时，

the existing tram network, which was considered outmoded and fit for demolition. In contrast to this, we were also shown the project of a modern underground system, which was the goal. We succeeded in restoring faith in the tram — provided it was modernised. Two technical delegations from Dalian visited Zurich; even the Lord Mayor became sufficiently interested to visit Zurich. At the end of the visit he declared that his trip to Zurich had convinced him that a modern tram line was the most appropriate transportation system for the city of Dalian. Dalian would begin to concentrate its energies on the modernisation and expansion of the existing tram network.

It turned out that these words were meant seriously, for their intention was implemented with extraordinary vigour: in October 2000, on another trip for expert talks in Dalian, approximately six kilometres of finished, new tracks and approximately twelve kilometres of tram line extension to a new suburb could be viewed, and we were given a demonstration of a modern low-floor-

articulated tram, designed and built in Dalian! The seeds sown in Kunming had ger-
minated in Dalian: the reintroduction of the
modern tram in China as a shining example
to other cities.

看到约6公里长的轨道已改造完毕，还
建设了近12公里长的、延伸至郊区的
新轨道。大连方面甚至还请我们参观
了现代化的低地板、铰接式有轨电车，
它是大连市自己设计并制造的！在昆
明播下的种子，在大连苗壮成长起来:
大连市在中国成功地建设起了现代化
的有轨电车网络，它是其它城市的光
辉榜样！

New tram tracks in Dalian.   大连市新建的电车轨道。

Improving 改善

the living conditions 这一代

of future generations　和子孙后代

and today's people 生活条件，

is the main goal of the　是中瑞双方

comprehensive co-operation 专家

of politicians 和政府领导之间

and experts from 展开全面合作的

China and Switzerland.   主要目标。

Co-operation across different cultures can lead to extraordinary solutions.
不同文化间的合作会产生不同寻常的解决方案。

DOMINIQUE DREYER　周铎勉

A Partnership Born out of China's Reform Policy　在中国的改革开放政策下诞生的友好城市关系

The partnership between Kunming and Zurich started at a crucial moment in the recent history of China. Twenty years ago, China was just emerging from almost 30 years of at times very unhappy history. When China opened up, following the policy of reforms initiated by Deng Xiaoping, it was as if the west rediscovered China. The establishment of formal diplomatic relations with the United States in 1979 was an important and symbolic step demonstrating the eagerness of the Chinese authorities to develop links with the rest of the world. In China itself, a huge need was felt to re-establish with the developed world ties which had been practically cut for almost 30 years, for the Chinese quickly realised that they needed to know more about the outside world. This awakened great expectations both in China and in the west, and it was felt everywhere that China was embarking on a new phase of its development and history. China was still regarded as a distant country shrouded in mystery, and her efforts at opening and reform were greeted with enormous sympathy everywhere. It was in this climate that the partnership between Kunming and Zurich started. It came at a very early stage of China's opening to the outside world and bears testimony to the

当昆明市与苏黎世市缔结友好城市关系之时，中国正处于当代历史上一个极为关键的转折点。二十年前，中国刚刚走出近三十年的黯淡阴影，在邓小平的领导下实行改革开放政策，面目一新，令西方国家感觉似乎重新发现了中国。1979年，中美正式建交，这一充满象征意义的重大事件也显示了中国政府与世界各国加强往来的愿望。在中国国内，人们渴望着与发达国家重拾中断了近三十年的联系，因为中国人民很快便发现，他们必须更多地了解世界。所有这一切，都唤醒了中国和西方国家的巨大期望。在任何地方都可以感受到，中国正迈入一个崭新的发展阶段和一个全新的历史时期。在西方国家眼里，中国仍然笼罩着一层神秘的面纱，她在改革开放方面所作的努力获得了世界各国的高度赞赏。正是在这个大环境下，昆明市与苏黎世市结成了友好城市。当时中国尚处于对外开放的初期，友好城市关系的建立，证明了昆明市和苏黎世市有关领导的远见卓识。

求同存异，成功合作

昆明市与苏黎世市的友好关系从一开始便须逾越许多障碍。两市相隔万里，语言迥异，但这并不是造成障碍的唯一原因。我们两国有着不同的政治制度，两市政府部门的组织原则也不尽相同。昆明市政府是中国国家行政管理体系的一部分，这一行政体系源于中国的悠久历史，它采用中央集权制，由中国共产党一党领导。苏黎世市政府则产生于瑞士广泛民主的深厚传统。这两种不同的政治体制会不会成为障碍，阻碍两市之间进行对话和建立非官方的、非政府性的关系呢？障碍总是可以克服的，虽然有时觉得"山重水复疑无路"，但是，只要双方愿意跨越这些障碍，便会"柳暗花明又一村"，达到更大的发展和更多的成功。两市正是抱着这种观念建立了友好城市关系，过去二十年的交往和合作也正是实现了这一观念。

两市之间的另一个重大差异，自然是经济发展状况的不同。云南省是中国一个经济不很发达的省份，但我不认为它属于中国最贫困的省份。云南省有着众多的民族，各族文化多姿多彩；云南省的自然风光神奇优美，旖旎动人；云南省的气候也是千变万化，无奇不有。过去，人们觉得云南是中国的偏远地区，而现在，人们认识到它座落在一条至关重要的交通要道上，通过这条交通要道上的泰国和越南，中国与东南亚山水相连。今后，云南省距东南亚经济发展最迅猛的几个地区将只有咫尺之遥，这将为云南省和昆明市带来巨大的发展机遇。

友好城市关系的新篇章

友好城市关系一般都仅限于官方代表团互访而已。而苏黎世在与昆明交往的过程中，却合作完成了不少非常有意义的项目。我认为这应归功于两市有关领导的探索精神和巨大努力。昆明在苏黎世的协助下制订了一系列环

vision and foresight of its promoters, both in Kunming and in Zurich.

Success despite difficulties

The partnership between Kunming and Zurich had to overcome a number of obstacles from the start. These were not all caused by the geographical distance and the language barrier. Not only are the political systems in our two countries very different, but the local authorities are also organised based on different principles. The local government of Kunming is part of an administrative system resulting from a long history and characterised by centralisation and control by a single political party. The Zurich municipal government is ruled by the long tradition of wide-open democracy in Switzerland. Should the differences between these two systems be an obstacle to dialogue and to the establishment of relations of a non-official and non-governmental nature between the two towns? Obstacles are there to be overcome, and if there is goodwill on both sides, overcoming them will make them springboards for further developments and further success. This is what was understood with the establishment of this partnership, and this is what was essentially realized over the course of these two decades.

Another important difference between the two towns is, of course, the difference in economic development. The province of Yunnan remains one of the less developed areas in China, but I would hesitate very much to say that it is one of the poorest. Yunnan Province is endowed with the rich culture of its many ethnic groups, it is endowed with spectacular landscapes, and furthermore, it has a great variety of climates. Yunnan used to be a backwater in China, but it is now situated on a very important axis that links

China to Southeast Asia through Thailand and Vietnam. In the years to come, Yunnan Province will be close to the centre of some of the most dynamic economies of Southeast Asia, and this will prove an important stimulus for the province and for Kunming.

A new turn in the partnership

Partnership relations between cities often do not go beyond the mere exchange of official delegations. I think that it is proof of the creativity and dynamism of their promoters that Zurich has engaged in some interesting projects in their relations with Kunming. The environmental projects developed in Kunming with the help of Zurich have contributed to water sanitation in Kunming, an acute problem that still has not been solved. But most of all, it is in the field of town planning and urban traffic management that the collaboration between the two towns has been most productive, to such an extent that Kunming has become a model city in China as regards urban traffic. The contribution of Zurich has been achieved with fairly limited resources, but the intellectual gain it represents goes far beyond that. Not only could Zurich base its close co-operation with Kunming on the solid basis of trust gained through the partnership, it also initiated an intensive series of seminars on water sanitation and on urban planning that served as an important tool for the exchange of knowledge and experiences. In this respect, this partnership strikes me as being without parallel in China. The partnership has also helped to

境项目，改善了昆明的供水和排水状况，这一任务仍然十分艰巨，可谓任重而道远。在所有合作项目中，两市在城市规划和城市交通领域的合作是最富有成效的。昆明市通过这个项目，成为中国在城市交通方面的典范。尽管苏黎世方面的项目资金相当有限，苏黎世仍为这个项目作出了巨大贡献，项目成果的精神价值是难以估量的。

Joseph Estermann, Mayor of Zurich and Chen Xinghua, Head of the Kunming Planning and Design Institute.
苏黎世市长约瑟夫·艾斯特曼与昆明规划院院长陈兴华。

两市通过友好城市关系建立了相互间的信任，为合作打下了坚实的基础。苏黎世市不但得以在这一基础上与昆明市展开密切合作，还在较短的时间里发起了一系列研讨会，这些关于供水和城市规划的研讨会成为交流知识和经验的重要手段。从这个意义上讲，我认为这种友好城市关系在中国是独一无二的。友好城市关系也推动瑞士有关方面在昆明和云南建立了许多有利的关系，这些关系使瑞士受益匪浅，它们蕴含着无比巨大的潜力，必将在今后发挥更为巨大的作用。

苏黎世和瑞士从与昆明市的友好关系中赢得了什么呢？人们首先想到的，自然是古色古香的苏黎世"中国园"。然而，瑞士和苏黎世所赢得的绝不仅于此。苏黎世是瑞士的第一大经济城市，友好城市关系把它的声望传播到了万里之外一个拥有巨大发展潜力的地区。苏黎世为瑞士打开了一扇大门，建立了一系列具有深远影响的关系。

领导和信念是不可或缺的

本实例证明，如此成功的友好城市关系离不开参与人员的坚定信心和政府领导的大力支持。正是出于双方的坚定信念，才使苏黎世与昆明的友好关系不但硕果累累，而且内容丰富多采。我相信，如果苏黎世第一副市长托马斯·瓦格纳博士不倾注这样巨大的热情，如果他的工作人员不付出这样执着的努力，友好城市关系无疑不会取得如此重大的发展。然而，最重要的是，友好关系获得了苏黎世市民的广泛支持。2000年11月市民投票公决的结果表明，广大市民赞同友好城市关系的作用和目标。因此可以说，友好城市关系也是民众通过民主方式表达的意愿。而这也是友好关系必须继续发展和深化下去的一个重要原因。

develop a network of very useful relationships for Switzerland in Kunming and in Yunnan. Its potential is still significant and is far from being exhausted.

What has the partnership with Kunming brought to Zurich and Switzerland? Of course, what comes to mind first is the quaint Chinese Garden in Zurich. But the benefits from this partnership do not stop there. Zurich being the main metropolis in Switzerland, the partnership has projected its image in a faraway region, in a region, however, which has immense potential. For Switzerland, Zurich has opened up a network of relationships of lasting importance.

Need for leadership and conviction

This example shows that such partnerships must be based on the determination of convinced individuals and political leaders. It is this strong conviction that has also made the partnership with Kunming not only successful but also so interesting in its content. There is no doubt in my mind that without the enthusiasm of Vice-President Dr. Thomas Wagner and the convinced dedication of his collaborators the partnership would not have developed the way it has. But, most of all, the partnership could be based finally on the popular support of the people of Zurich. The result of the referendum of November 2000 has shown a broad agreement with the purpose and the objectives of the partnership. This partnership can thus also be seen as a lesson of democracy, and this is one of the reasons why it should continue and develop even further.

Yang Jianqiang, Party Secretary of Kunming and Thomas Wagner, First Deputy Mayor of Zurich, planting a tree of friendship. 昆明市委书记杨健强和苏黎世第一副市长托马斯·瓦格纳合种友谊树。

Thomas Wagner, First Deputy Mayor of Zurich, and Zhang Zhen-guo, Mayor of Kunming. 托马斯·瓦格纳与昆明市市长章振国。

ZHANG ZHENGUO, MAYOR OF KUNMING　章振国，昆明市市长

Co-operation and Sustainable Urban Development

加强合作交流，推动城市可持续发展

Sustainable Urban Development has become a vitally important issue facing countries around the world in the modernisation process. The co-operation between Kunming and Zurich on urban development issues has built a successful example for sustainable development.

A friendly tie between the Swiss city of Zurich and the southern Chinese city of Kunming was established in 1982. Mutual efforts to co-operate in urban planning, city construction and cultural exchange were made. Since 1994 especially, the two cities have engaged in fruitful and constructive co-operation in multiple fields of sustainable urban development and public transportation planning, including the selection of patterns of city development space and a comprehensive public transportation system, as well as water supply and waste water treatment. The City of Zurich provided Kunming with valuable support in project planning, technology and finance. In addition, the two cities successfully held three Sino-Swiss Sustainable Urban Development and Public Transportation Planning Symposia: in 1996, 1999 and 2001. These achieved good results, gave a consid-

可持续发展是现代化历程中世界各国面临的共同课题。昆明市与瑞士苏黎世市在城市建设领域所开展的富有成效的合作交流，为促进可持续发展树立了成功的典范。

自1982年昆明市与瑞士苏黎世市缔结友好城市后，双方在城市规划、城市建设和文化等方面，开展了广泛的合作交流。尤其是自1994年以来，双方在城市可持续发展与公共交通规划，以及城市发展空间模式选择、综合性公共交通体系、供水及污水处理等诸多领域的合作，取得了实质性成果。苏黎世市在项目规划和技术、资金等方面，给予了昆明十分可贵的帮助和支持。与此同时，双方还分别在1996年、1999年和2001年，成功地组织了三届"中瑞城市可持续发展及公共交通规划研讨会"，产生了良好效应，有力地推动了昆明城市规划的进步，使可持续发展深入人心。

本书完整地反映了这两座来自不同国度和文化背景的城市，在城市可持续发展和交通政策领域二十年来的成功合作。我们希望通过本书向其它城市和各界人士介绍，我们是怎样努力实

现城市可持续发展、可持续交通规划和交通政策的。昆明市与苏黎世市合作项目的成功实践证明，积极探索有效的合作途径，广泛学习借鉴先进技术和成功经验，不仅有助于我们开阔视野，不断丰富规划、建设和管理城市的手段，同时，也必将进一步推进中国城市实现经济、生态和社会三者协调发展。

erable boost to the progress of Kunming's city planning, and thus firmly planted the idea of sustainable development in the hearts of people.

This book documents a success story of 20 years of joint work, conducted by two cities from two different countries and with totally different cultures, in the interest of sustainable urban development and transportation policies. We would like to show other cities and peoples how we have made efforts to attain a successful sustainable urban development and transportation planning policy. The Kunming collaboration project is proof that the active search for effective co-operation, the learning of modern technology, and shared experience have not only helped us to widen our thoughts and to enrich our urban planning, urban construction and urban management methods, but will also promote balanced economic, ecological, and social success in Chinese cities.

THOMAS WAGNER, FIRST DEPUTY MAYOR, CITY OF ZURICH

托马斯·瓦格纳，苏黎世市第一副市长

Aims and Successes of a City Partnership 友好城市关系的目标和成果

The economy of Kunming has surged over the past two decades. Unfortunately, as a consequence, air and water quality has deteriorated rapidly. As the economy grew, new transportation needs arose. To meet this challenge, Kunming began promoting the use of motorcars by building new highways, banning bicycles and clearing intersections of pedestrians. At the same time, suburban sprawl spread over the rural areas surrounding Kunming. Mainly flat areas with the most fertile soils were misused for urban development.

At quite an early stage, the City Government took notice of its Sister City Zurich's different and successful urban development and transportation policy, and asked Zurich for support in a planning process for similar development in Kunming. The City Government of Zurich agreed, and the Swiss Agency for Development and Co-operation, part of the Swiss Central Government, was ready to help as well, aiming to create a pilot project in China. With this support, Kunming changed direction. In an outstanding case of Chinese – Swiss co-operation, a quest for a better city began. This book gives an overview of the results. What are the most decisive reasons for this project's outstanding success?

- The long-term city partnership created

在过去二十年里，昆明市的经济取得了长足发展。遗憾的是，飞速发展的经济也使得空气质量和水质迅速下降。随着经济的发展，出现了对交通运输的新需求。为了满足这一新需求，昆明市修建了许多高速公路、限制自行车交通，并取消了不少交叉路口的人行道，以推动机动车的发展。同时，高楼林立的建成区向昆明城区周围的农村地区蔓延，这些地区大都是肥沃而平坦的良田，却被城市建设活动蚕食掉了。

昆明市政府在很早的时候就认识到，其姐妹城市苏黎世市采用的是另一种城市发展及交通政策，并取得了成功。因此，昆明市请苏黎世市对昆明的规划工作给予支持，以实现类似的发展。苏黎世市政府欣然同意，瑞士联邦政府发展与合作司也愿意提供帮助，使这个项目成为在中国的一个试点项目。在这一支持下，昆明市改变了它原来的方针。中瑞双方展开了优异合作，共同探索如何把昆明市建设得更加美好。本书概括总结了本项目迄今为止取得的成果。合作能够取得如此令人瞩目的成就，主要应归功于下列因素：

- 多年的友好城市关系，使双方各有关方面树立起了信心，建立起了友谊，这

213

是双方能够开诚布公讨论问题的前提。

- 早在1987年，双方就展开了供水和排水方面的合作项目，成功地进行了合作。
- 中方的领导和官员访问了苏黎世和欧洲其它城市，考察了可持续发展的成功范例。
- 昆明市政府下定决心，要以可持续的方式建设昆明市，把昆明市建设成为一座富裕的、健康的、社会各方面均衡发展的城市。
- 在制订各个项目的整个过程中，中瑞双方专家们自始至终都展开了密切合作，把发达国家的经验与中国的国情结合在了一起。
- 在瑞士方面，苏黎世市政府的官员极富日常工作经验，了解如何实际操作项目；瑞士联邦工业大学则是瑞士最优秀的理工科学府，它的专家们通晓该领域中最先进的科学方法。这两方面的人员携手合作，为合作项目奠定了理想的基础。
- 昆明方面乐于接触并了解新知识，愿意学习许多国外城市的解决方案，并具有取其精华洋为中用的能力。
- 昆明市政府拥有政治上的勇气，敢于实施在中国尚无前例的新型优秀项目。

confidence, even friendship, between the responsible parties on both sides, as a pre-condition for open discussion of issues and ideas.
- Previously, in 1987, a collaborative project in the field of water supply and sewage had been very successful.
- Chinese leaders and officers visited Zurich and other European cities, to study examples of more sustainable solutions.
- The Kunming City Government had a strong desire to develop their city in a sustainable way: to become a rich city, to become a healthy city, to became a socially well-balanced city.
- Chinese and Swiss experts worked closely together, mixing experience from developed countries with Chinese customs during the whole process of elaborating different projects.
- On the Swiss side, the joint workforce of city officers, experienced at putting projects into practice from their daily work, along with experts from the Swiss Federal Institute of Technology, the most respected technical university in Switzerland, able to offer the most advanced scientific approaches in the field, created an ideal basis for the collaboration work.
- On the Kunming side, there was a positive attitude, open minds ready to accept new knowledge, willingness to study solutions from many cities abroad, and a finely honed ability to extract the essential, the feasible, for use at home.
- Political courage on the part of the City Government of Kunming to undertake new, outstanding projects, never before seen in China.

Appendix 附录

Illustrations 图片

China Kunming International Tourism Festival, Dong Feng Square, April 2000 中国昆明国际旅游节，东风广场，2000年4月

Guandu, traditional opera, 1999 官渡古镇内的戏楼，1999年

Business area near the former south gate of Kunming, 2001 昆明南城门原址附近的商业区，2001年

Wu Cheng Road, 1996 武成路，1996年 Areas north of the old town, 1996 旧城北部地区，1996年

Between Dong Feng and Jinbi Road, 1997 东风路与金碧路之间，1997年

Anning, 2001 安宁市，2001年

North Town, urban design concept, 1997 北市区，城市设计方案，1997年

North Town, 2002 北市区，2002年

Expo 99 99世博会

Old town, Wenmin area, 2002
旧城内的文明街片区，2002年

Old town 1997 – 1999
旧城，1997年至1999年间

Reconstruction near Bajita Road,
2002　白塔路附近的古建筑修复工程，
2002年　Old town 1996　旧城，
1996年

Tenway Shopping Centre, 1997
天元商厦，1997年

Residential area in the southern
part of Kunming, 2001　昆明南部的
居住小区，2001年

City Planning Administration, Vice
Mayor Mr. Hu Xing, Vice Mayor
Dr. Thomas Wagner and staff mem-
bers, 2001　昆明市规划局，胡星副
市长、托马斯·瓦格纳副市长及工作人
员，2001年

View from landing airplane, in the
background the West Mountains,
2001　从即将降落的飞机上俯瞰昆
明，背景为西山，2001年

Lake Dian, eastern shore near
Chenggong, 1997　滇池，呈贡附近
的滇池东岸，1997年

North of Kunming, 1997　昆明北
部1997年

217

Plain between Kunming and Lake Dian, 1998　昆明与滇池之间的平原，1998年

School children on the way home, near a village north of Kunming, 1997　放学回家的学生。昆明北部的一座村落附近，1997年

Guandu in ancient times. Painting of an older inhabitant of Guandu, 2000　官渡古貌。官渡一位老人的绘画，2000年

Guandu, Stupa in the central part of the town, 2002　官渡，古镇中心的金刚塔，2002年

2nd Ring Road East, 1998
东二环路，1998年

Kunming southeast, 1999　昆明东南部，1999年　Anning – Caopu, 2001　安宁 – 草铺，2001年

Satellite town between Kunming and Yanglin, urban design vision, 2002　昆明与杨林之间的卫星城，城市设计构想，2002年

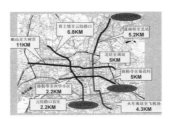

Planning for four modern bus lanes, 2000 (picture: Kunming Planning and Design Institute)
四条现代化公共交通专用道的规划，2000年。（本图由昆明市规划院提供）

Beijing Road, 1998　北京路，1998年　Dushupu station, between Kunming and Anning, 2001　位于昆明与安宁之间的读书铺火车站，2001年

Dong Feng Road, 1997
东风路，1997年

Experimental bus line in a
reserved lane. Dong Feng Road,
1995 实验性的公交专用道。东风
路，1995年

Experimental bus line in a
reserved lane. Dong Feng Road,
1995 实验性的公交专用道。东风
路，1995年

Beijing Road, 2001
北京路，2001年

Modernised tram track in Dalian,
Liaoning Province, 2000 辽宁省
大连市经过现代化改造的有轨电车轨
道，2000年

Train station Kunming North, 1997
北客站，1997年

North Town, near long distance
bus station, 2002 北市区，长途汽
车站附近，2002年

Near Kunming Airport, 1998 昆明
机场附近，1998年

Jinbi Road, 2002 金碧路，2002年

Central Business District, 1996
中心商业区，1996年

Experts meet in Guandu, 2000
专家们在官渡考察，2000年

Signing contracts for co-operation,
1999　签署合作项目，1999年

Chinese and Swiss experts, 1998
中瑞双方的专家，1998年

Experts in the renovated Jin Lan
tea house in the old town, 2002
专家们在老城内维修一新的金兰茶
苑，2002年

Night over Kunming, Panlong river
area, 2000　昆明夜景，盘龙江地
区，2000年

Authors

Dreyer, Dominique
Born in 1945, Lic. Jur. (Fribourg),
LLB.Cantab., Dr. Jur. (Fribourg).
In the Swiss diplomatic service
since 1972, at present Ambassa-
dor of Switzerland to China.

Fingerhuth, Carl
Born in 1936. Self-employed
architect in Zurich with an emphasis on urban planning, 1979–
1992 Director of Building in
Basle, Professor at the Technical
University of Darmstadt, Germany.

Feiner, Jacques
Born in 1962, Dr. ès. sc. techn,
Dipl. Arch. ETH, Planner ETH-NDS,
senior researcher at the ORL-
Institute of the Swiss Federal
Institute of Technology Zurich,
project manager of the Training
and Research Project 'Regional
Development Kunming'.

Gao Xuemei
Born in 1968, B. Eng. from
Chongqing Architecture University
in Chongqing. Senior urban planner at the Kunming Urban Planning and Design Institute.

Gou Jinsuo
Born in 1952, degree from Yunnan
Radio and Television University.
Vice Director of the Kunming Rail-
way Administration.

Hu Xing
Born in 1958, B. Eng. from
Chongqing Architecture University
in Chongqing. Vice Mayor of the
Kunming Municipal Government.

Joos, Ernst
Born in 1935, Dipl. Ing. ETH/SIA,
Deputy Director of the Transport
Authority Zurich, Project Man-
ager of the 'Urban Development
Kunming – Masterplan Public
Transport' Project.

Krähenbühl, Hans Rudolf
Born in 1934, Ing. chem. ETH,
Department of Construction,
Waste Disposal and Sewage Zur-
ich, Assistant General Manager of
Sewage Division.

Lin Wei
Born in 1966, M. Eng. and B.
Eng. from Tsinghua University in
Beijing. Deputy Chief Engineer
of Kunming Urban Planning and
Design Institute.

Liu Xue
Born in 1958, M. Eng. and B. Eng.
from Tongji University in Shanghai. Director General of Kunming
Urban Planning Authority and
Director of Kunming Urban Planning and Design Institute.

Louy, Oliver
Born in 1959, Dipl. Master of Sci-
ence from University of Montreal,
Researcher and GIS manager at
the Division of Landscape and En-
vironmental Planning (LEP) of the
Insitute of National, Regional and
Local Planning (ORL) at the Swiss
Federal Institute of Technology
(ETH).

Mi Shiwen
Born in 1966, Postgraduate
Diploma NDS ETHZ. B. Eng. from
Tongji University in Shanghai.
Deputy Director of the Municipal
Infrastructure Planning Depart-
ment of the Kunming Urban Plan-
ning Authority.

Salmeron, Diego
Born in 1969, Dipl. Ing. ETH, Re-
searcher at the Division of Land-
scape and Environmental Planning
(LEP) of the Institute of National,
Regional and Local Planning (ORL)
at the Swiss Federal Institute of
Technology (ETH).

Schmid, Willy A.
Born in 1943, Professor for Rural
Engineering and Planning, Head
of the Division of Landscape and
Environmental Planning (LEP)
of the Institute of National, Regional and Local Planning (ORL)
at the Swiss Federal Institute of
Technology (ETH).

Stutz, Werner
Born in 1942, Dr.phil. Architectural Historian, Vice Director of
Protection of Historic Monuments
and Archaeology for the City of
Zurich, since 1971 expert on the
protection of historic monuments,
1992–1996 teaching post at the
University of Zurich.

Tang Chong
Born in 1942, Civil Engineer at
the Kunming Urban Planning and
Design Institute.

Traber, Markus
Born in 1965, MSc. Civil Engi-
neering ETH, Electrowatt Infra
Ltd., Head of Traffic and Railway
Section, Chief Resident Engineer
in Kunming 1996–98, Project
Manager for Traffic Planning and
Engineering since 1999.

Wagner, Thomas
Born in 1943, Dr. med. Dr. iur.,
1982–1990 Mayor of the City
of Zurich. Up to May 2002:
First Deputy Mayor of the City
of Zurich, and political leader
responsible for the collaboration
projects with Kunming.

Wang Xuehai
Born in 1968, B. Eng. from Tongji
University in Shanghai. Senior
urban planner. Deputy Director of
the Kunming Urban Planning and
Design Institute.

Wehrlin, Matthias
Born in 1945, Architect/Urban
Planner FSU/SIA/SWB, Inde-
pendent Urban Planner in Bern.
1972–1979: Collaboration in
Atelier 5 Bern, 1979–2001: Col-
laboration in the City Planning
Department, Bern.

Zhang Zhenguo
Born in 1948, Bachelor's degree
from Yunnan University. Mayor of
Kunming Municipal Government.

Zhou Jie
Born in 1961. B. Eng. from China
University of Mining & Technol-
ogy. Senior urban planner. First
Deputy Director of the Kunming
Urban Planning and Design Insti-
tute.

Zimmermann, Ulrich
Born in 1937, Dr.sc.nat., Federal
Institute of Technology, Zurich
(ETHZ), Deputy General Director,
Zurich Water Supply, Project Man-
ager of the Collaboration between
Kunming Water Supply and Zurich
Water Supply.

作者名录

周铎勉
生于1945年，瑞士弗利堡大学法学硕士、英国剑桥大学法学学士、瑞士弗利堡大学法学博士。自1972年起在瑞士外交部工作，现任瑞士驻华大使。

卡尔•芬格胡特
生于1936年，瑞士苏黎世独立建筑师，主要从事城市规划。1979年至1992年间曾任瑞士巴塞尔州政府建设厅长，德国达姆施塔特工业大学教授。

雅克•菲恩纳
生于1962年，瑞士联邦工业大学技术科学博士、建筑学硕士、规划师。现任瑞士联邦工业大学国土、区域及城市规划学院高级研究员，并任培训及研究项目"昆明区域发展项目"的负责人。

高雪梅
生于1968年，重庆建筑大学学士。昆明城市规划设计研究院高级城市规划师。

苟金锁
生于1952年，毕业于云南广播电视大学。昆明铁路局副局长。

胡星
生于1958年，重庆建筑大学学士。昆明市政府副市长。

恩斯特•约斯
生于1935年，瑞士联邦工业大学硕士工程师，瑞士建筑师及工程师协会成员。苏黎世市交通局副局长，"昆明城市发展与公共交通总体规划"项目负责人。

汉斯•鲁道夫•克莱恩比尔
生于1934年，瑞士联邦工业大学化学工程师。现任苏黎世市政府工程局废物及污水处理分局污水处理部总经理助理。

林卫
生于1966年，清华大学学士及硕士。昆明城市规划设计研究院副总工程师。

刘学
生于1958年，同济大学学士及硕士。昆明市规划局局长、昆明城市规划设计研究院院长。

奥利弗•路易
生于1959年，蒙特利尔大学科学硕士。现任瑞士联邦工业大学国土、区域及城市规划学院景观及环境规划部研究员兼地理信息系统GIS管理员。

米世文
生于1966年，获瑞士联邦工业大学后学士学位。同济大学学士。昆明市规划局市政规划处副处长。

迪哥•萨尔美隆
生于1969年，瑞士联邦工业大学硕士工程师。瑞士联邦工业大学国土、区域及城市规划学院景观及环境规划部研究员。

威利•A•施密特
生于1943年，农业工程与规划教授。瑞士联邦工业大学国土、区域及城市规划学院景观及环境规划部主任。

威尔纳•施图茨
生于1942年，建筑历史学博士。苏黎世市文物及考古局常务副局长。自1971年起任文物保护问题专家，1992年至1996年间任苏黎世大学讲师。

唐翀
生于1942年。昆明城市规划设计研究院土木工程师。

马库斯•特拉伯
生于1965年，瑞士联邦工业大学土木工程师、硕士。现任瓦特公司交通及铁路部部门经理。1996年至1998年间任瓦特公司常驻昆明首席工程师，自1999年起任交通规划及工程设计项目负责人。

托马斯•瓦格纳
生于1943年，医学博士、法学博士。1982年至1990年任苏黎世市长。至2002年5月任苏黎世市第一副市长，并任苏黎世与昆明合作项目的政府负责人。

王学海
生于1968年，同济大学学士。高级城市规划师。昆明城市规划设计研究院副院长。

玛提亚斯•魏尔林
生于1945年，瑞士国家级建筑师及城市规划师。瑞士伯尔尼独立城市规划师。1972年至1979年间在伯尔尼的Atelier 5公司工作，1979年至2001年间任职于伯尔尼市规划部门。

章振国
生于1948年，云南大学学士。昆明市政府市长。

周杰
生于1961年，中国矿业大学学士。高级城市规划师。昆明城市规划设计研究院常务副院长。

乌尔里希•齐默尔曼
生于1937年，瑞士联邦工业大学自然科学博士。苏黎世市供水局副局长，昆明自来水公司与苏黎世供水局合作项目负责人。

Bibliography 参考文献

Booklets concerning special items in the frame of the Zurich – Kunming co-operation project. Editor: Industrielle Betriebe der Stadt Zürich 与昆明－苏黎世合作项目中各课题有关的参考文献。
主编：苏黎世市公共工业局

Master Plan for Public Transport, Executive Summary, 1996 1996 《公共交通总体规划内容摘要》，1996年

Regional Development and Rapid Short Range Passenger Railway, 2000 《区域发展与快速短途客运铁路》，2000年

Rapid Short Range Passenger Railway for the Greater Kunming Area, 1999 《大昆明区的快速短途客运铁路》，1999年

Urban Landscape Planning Report, 1996 《城市景观规划报告》，1996年

Urban Landscape Planning Report, 1997 《城市景观规划报告》，1997年

Urban Landscape Planning Report, 1998 《城市景观规划报告》，1998年

巴西库利提巴市，1996年

《现代化的城市交通政策》，1997年

Demonstration Bus Line, 1998 《公共汽车示范线》，1998年

Technical Study for the first LRT Line, 1999 《轻轨一号线技术研究》，1999年

Old Town Kunming, Methodical Protection Manual, 2000 昆明旧城的《保护方法手册》，2000年

Urban Landscape Planning, Gao Shan Pu & Gao Shan Xi Lu Areas, 2001 《高山铺和华山西路片区的城市景观规划》，2001年

Guandu Historical Town Protection and Modern Development, 2001 《官渡古镇的保护和现代化开发》，2001年

Lake Dian East Shore Development, 2001 《滇池东岸的开发》，2001年

Priority for Pedestrians, October, 2001 《行人优先》，2001年10月

Anning, Strategies for Sustainable Development, 2002 《安宁市的可持续发展策略》，2002年

Rapid Short Range Passenger Services from Kunming to Anning and Yuxi, 2002 《从昆明至安宁及玉溪的快速短途客运服务》，2002年

Kunming East; Strategies for Sustainable Development, January 2002 《昆明东市区的可持续发展策略》，2002年1月

Bericht des Stadtrates von Zürich zur Städtepartnerschaft 1982–1999, 1999 《苏黎世市政府关于友好城市关系（1982－1999）的报告》，1999年

Städtepartnerschaft Zürich – Kunming; ein beispielhaftes Pilotprojekt, 2001

City Partnership Zurich – Kunming; an exemplary pilot study, 2001 《昆明市与苏黎世市的友好城市关系：堪称楷模的先导性项目》，2001年

Swiss Federal Institute of Technology, ORL-Institute, Zurich (Ed); Greater Kunming Area, Regional Development Scenarios, 2000 位于苏黎世的瑞士联邦工业大学国土、区域及城市规划学院（主编）：《大昆明区的区域发展前景》，2000年

Schweizer Ingenieur und Architekt, SI+A (Ed), Sondernummer China, Nr. 48/1998 瑞士工程师及建筑师协会，会刊SI+A（主编）：《中国特刊》，1998年第48期

英文翻译
  卡洛琳娜•阿伦丝，德国汉堡
中文翻译:
  王维，瑞士苏黎世
平面设计:
  弗兰希丝卡•肖特与马可•希比克设计公司，
  瑞士伯尔尼
英中文排版:
  玛丽安娜•赛乐，瑞士伯尔尼
英文审校:
  苏珊•詹姆斯，加拿大多伦多
中文审校:
  米世文，中国昆明

摄影师
  封面及摄影精选: 玛提亚斯•魏尔林，伯尔尼;
  恩斯特•约斯，苏黎世 (第144-147页，第150-151)
  其它照片: 米夏埃尔•波利，苏黎世;
  卡尔•芬格胡特，苏黎世; 弗洛里安•胡根托布勒，
  苏黎世; 恩斯特•约斯，苏黎世; 莱纳•克罗斯特曼，
  苏黎世; 威尔纳•施图茨博士，苏黎世; 斯特拉斯
  堡市; 马库斯•特拉伯，苏黎世; 玛提亚斯•魏尔林，
  伯尔尼; 卡琳•冯•魏特斯海姆－柯拉玛斯塔，苏黎世;
  苏黎世市交通局; 赵辰教授、博士，南京;
  乌尔里希•齐默尔曼博士，苏黎世

English translation:
  Caroline Ahrens, Hamburg/D
Chinese translation:
  Wei Grueber-Wang, Zurich/CH
Graphic design:
  Franziska Schott & Marco Schibig, Bern/CH
English and Chinese Typesetting:
  Marianne Seiler, Bern/CH
English Copy editing:
  Susan James, Toronto/CA
Chinese copy editing:
  Shiwen Mi, Kunming/PRC

Photographers
  Cover and photo essays : Matthias Wehrlin, Bern;
  Ernst Joos, Zurich (pages 144-147, 150-151)
  Others: Michael Bolli, Zurich; Carl Fingerhuth,
  Zurich; Florian Hugentobler, Zurich; Ernst Joos,
  Zurich; Rainer Klostermann, Zurich; Dr. Werner
  Stutz, Zurich; City of Strasbourg; Markus Traber,
  Zurich; Matthias Wehrlin, Bern; Karin von Wieters-
  heim-Kramsta, Zurich; Verkehrsbetriebe Zurich;
  Prof. Dr. Zhao Chen, Nanjing; Dr. Ulrich
  Zimmermann, Zurich

A CIP catalogue record for this book is available from the Library of Congress, Washington D.C., USA.

Die Deutsche Bibliothek – CIP-Einheitsaufnahme
The Kunming project – urban development in China : a dialogue / Hrsg. Carl Fingerhuth ; Ernst Joos im Auftr. der Städte Kunming und Zürich. Übers. Caroline Ahrens ; Wei Grueber-Wang. – Boston ; Basel ; Berlin : Birkhäuser, 2002
ISBN 3-7643-6742-3

© 2002 Birkhäuser – Publishers for Architecture, P.O. Box 133, CH-4010 Basel, Switzerland
Member of the BertelsmannSpringer Publishing Group

本书使用全无氯纸浆生产的无酸纸印刷。

德国印刷
ISBN 3-7643-6742-3

9 8 7 6 5 4 3 2 1

www.birkhauser.ch

© 2002 Birkhäuser – Publishers for Architecture, P.O. Box 133, CH-4010 Basel, Switzerland
Member of the BertelsmannSpringer Publishing Group

Printed on acid-free paper produced from chlorine-free pulp. TCF ●

Printed in Germany
ISBN 3-7643-6742-3

9 8 7 6 5 4 3 2 1

www.birkhauser.ch